# English 1 Works

**John Catron,
Chris Marshall
and Jo Shackleton**

## Hodder & Stoughton

A MEMBER OF THE HODDER HEADLINE GROUP

**Copyright text:**
p. 4 © Faber & Faber; pp. 25, 28, 29, 30, 31, 32, 33, 34, 35, 36, 38, 40, 41 extracts from 'The Star Beast' published in *Mainly in the Moonlight* by Nicholas Stuart Gray © Faber and Faber Limited; pp. 52, 55, 59, 60, 63, 67 extracts from *Stop the Train* by Geraldine McCaughrean, published by Oxford University Press; p. 113 © *The New Internationalist* magazine, www.newint.org, interview by Jeremy Lennard; p. 124 © www.newint.org

**Copyright photographs:**
p. 11 (top left) © Graham Burns/Life File, (top right) © Emma Lee/Life File, (middle) © Jeremy Hoare/Life File, (bottom left) © Aubrey J Slaughter/Life File, (bottom right) © Andrew Ward/Life File; p. 14 (left) © Jeff Greenberg@uno.com, (right) © Steve Norgrove/Life File; p. 16 © Emma Lee/Life File; p. 47 © OUP; p. 49 © Transworld Publishers Ltd; p. 50 jacket illustration by Larry Rostant for *Stop the Train* by Geraldine McCaughrean (OUP, 2001), reprinted by permission of Oxford University Press; p. 54 © Bettmann/Corbis; p. 59 © Bettmann/Corbis; p. 62 © Bettmann/Corbis; p. 63 © John Copes Van Hasselt/CORBIS SYGMA; p. 65 © John Copes Van Hasselt/CORBIS SYGMA; p. 71 © Lake County Museum/Corbis; p. 72 © The Ronald Grant Archive; p. 81 © London Aerial Photo Library/CORBIS; p. 83 © Adam Woolfitt/CORBIS; p. 87 © Barry Mayes/Life File; p. 108 © The Image Bank/Getty Images; p. 110 © AP Photo/Pat Roque; p. 113 © John Bartholomew/Corbis; p. 116 © AP Photo/Richard Vogel; p. 117 © AP Photo/Beatrix Stampfli; p. 122 © AP Photo/Manish Swarup; p. 125 © Nicola Sutton/Life File; p. 139 © The Ronald Grant Archive; p. 145 © Donald Cooper/Photostage.

**Illustrations:**
pp. 1, 4, 6, 12, 19, 20, 22, 23, 27, 93, 95, 104, 109, 129, 131, 132, 136 by Ben Hasler.
pp. 21, 35, 45, 56, 61, 66, 73, 78, 84, 85, 90, 92, 143, 148, 150, 152 by Ruth Thomlevold.

**Contributors:**
Unit 1: Ruth Corrie and Sarah Speedle
Unit 2: John Catron
Unit 3: Annie Keighley
Unit 4: Denise Savage
Unit 5: Kathryn Burns
Unit 6: Julie Lewis
Unit 7: Maria Cox and Samantha Simpson
Unit 8: Jo Shackleton

Every effort has been made to trace copyright holders of material reproduced in this book. Any rights not acknowledged here will be acknowledged in subsequent printings if notice is given to the publisher.

Orders: please contact Bookpoint Ltd, 130 Milton Park, Abingdon, Oxon OX14 4SB. Telephone: (44) 01235 827720. Fax: (44) 01235 400454. Lines are open from 9.00–6.00, Monday to Saturday, with a 24 hour message answering service. You can also order through our website www.hodderheadline.co.uk.

*British Library Cataloguing in Publication Data*
A catalogue record for this title is available from the British Library

ISBN 0 340 87253 5

First Published 2003
Impression number    10 9 8 7 6 5 4 3 2 1
Year                         2007 2006 2005 2004 2003

Copyright © 2003 John Catron, Chris Marshall and Jo Shackleton

Cover photo from Jim Wehtje/Photodisc @ Getty Images.
Typeset by Pantek Arts Ltd, Maidstone, Kent, ME14 1NY.
Printed in Italy for Hodder & Stoughton Educational, a division of Hodder Headline, 338 Euston Road, London NW1 3BH.

# Contents

# UNIT 1 Terror Town

KEY OBJECTIVES

In this unit you will learn about the following key objectives:

**Stylistic conventions of non-fiction** (information, recount, explanation and instructions) – revising these text types by drawing out their features, identifying their conventions and considering their purpose and impact on a reader

**Organise texts appropriately** – using your knowledge and understanding to write in a range of these styles and organising your ideas in the most appropriate ways for your audience and purpose

The management at your local theme park, Terror Town, has decided that they need to attract more visitors next summer. To do this they have decided that a brand new ride is needed. It must be totally original and utterly terrifying. Linking it with the theme of Ancient Egypt is also part of the plan.

In this unit you are going to work in groups to act as a team of designers working on this project.

You will be required to **recount** your experience, **inform** the public, **instruct** visitors and **explain** your design to the management of Terror Town.

## Text types

Before you can begin work on your ride designs, you need to revise your understanding of some of the main non-fiction text types.

**TASK**

❶ Look at these text types:
1. Explanation
2. Information
3. Instructions
4. Recount

❷ Can you match them to the following examples?
- ❏ A recipe for a fruit cake
- ❏ A newspaper report
- ❏ The biography of a famous footballer
- ❏ A set of directions for travelling to a friend's house
- ❏ A geography textbook
- ❏ A computer manual
- ❏ An account of a historical event
- ❏ A school prospectus
- ❏ A letter from the headteacher to parents about arrangements for sports day
- ❏ A bank statement
- ❏ A sports commentary
- ❏ A guide book to Windsor Castle

❸ Some texts share the conventions of more than one text type. With a partner, discuss which of these examples might involve, for example, information **and** explanation or information **and** instructions. Share your ideas with the class.

In order to complete the next task, you will need to think about the language features of our four text types. It will help you to consider:

● The way the whole text is organised and set out
● The types of sentences used
● The types of words used

# TASK

Write the four text type headings on post-it notes or pieces of paper and place them on the desk in front of you. Now work with a partner to arrange the language features underneath the correct headings. You may find that some language features apply to more than one text and that some texts may use a number of different language features!

## Text types

1  Explanation
2  Information
3  Instructions
4  Recount

## Language features

● Factual, impersonal style
● Headings and sub-headings
● Tables and diagrams
● Glossary
● Third person
● Present tense
● Step-by-step sequence
● Past tense
● Active voice
● Passive voice
● Chronological order
● Technical vocabulary
● Plain vocabulary
● Connectives linked to cause and effect
● Connectives linked to comparison
● Connectives linked to sequence
● First person
● Mainly short, simple sentences
● Varied sentence structure and length
● Connectives linked to time
● Dates and places
● Adjectives, adverbs and powerful verbs
● Clear, direct style
● Imperative verbs
● Second person

On the next four pages, you will find examples of each text type. For each text, you will need to work with a partner to discuss the following:

❶ What text type is this?

❷ How do you know?

❸ Consider:
- ❏ Who it is written for (its audience)
- ❏ What it is written for (its purpose)
- ❏ Its language features (the checklist on page 3 will help you if necessary)

❹ After you've done this, write down five pieces of information this text provides.

---

Headings/ sub-headings to categorise information

Usually third person but first and second person here has effect of drawing reader in and creating chatty, conversational tone. Who might this book be aimed at?

# HIEROGLYPHS

General opening statement → The earliest Ancient Egyptian writing was the hieroglyphic script.

Present tense describes how things are

Hieroglyphs are what most of <u>us</u> think of when <u>we</u> talk about Ancient Egyptian writing. <u>It's</u> the picture writing <u>you'll</u> find on the walls of pharaohs' tombs, carved into ancient temple columns or written on the mummy cases of the dead. <u>It's</u> a useful language to be able to read if you're trying to avoid three-thousand-year-old curses, or trying to find out who's buried in that <u>sarcophagus</u> you <u>smuggled</u> out of a museum.

Vocabulary of precision, e.g. facts/ technical terms etc.

Length of sentence dictated by need to be clear; tendency towards simple and compound sentences

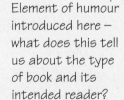

Element of humour introduced here – what does this tell us about the type of book and its intended reader?

*These Ancient Egyptian hieroglyphs spell out a single word of warning:*

Diagrams/ illustrations to assist reader

When writing with heiroglyphs, there's no punctuation to worry about – no full stops, commas, question marks, or anything like that. This makes it easier to write... but much harder to read, especially when there are no gaps between the words either!

Nouns and verbs predominate

Title ——— indicates how

Past tense ———

# HOW THE PYRAMIDS WERE BUILT

Time ——— connectives

Layout generally designed to make text appealing and easy to read

Numbered stages for clarity and sequence

1. One way of cutting stone blocks for a pryamid was to cut notches in solid rock and hammer in wooden wedges. When water was poured on the wedges, they swelled, splitting off the blocks cleanly.

2. Most of the massive blocks used to build the Great Pyramid were quarried in the desert nearby. The white stones used to form the outer layer were brought across the Nile from the east bank.

Sentences clear and unambiguous – the reader is not expected to infer or deduce

3. The ground where the pyramid was to be built had to be cleared of sand and stones. Workers dug long channels and filled them with water. When the water didn't run to one end, they knew the site was level.

4. The most difficult job of all was to raise the heavy stones into place. Most people think the stones were pulled up a huge earth ramp that was raised each time a new layer of stones was added.

Little technical vocabulary – text is probably aimed at children

Contains diagrams to aid clarity

5. When the pyramid was finished, the ramp was taken away layer by layer. As the ramp went down, workers put white blocks of limestone on the jagged sides of the pyramid, to give them a smooth outer surface.

6. After many years' work, the pyramid was ready. When the Pharaoh died, his coffin was dragged up to the burial chamber inside it. Then the way into the pyramid was blocked with stone slabs and hidden.

Passive voice – impersonal tone

Past tense since these are past events

# TASK

Read the text 'How the pyramids were built' and answer the following questions.

❶ How is this text different from the first one?

❷ Who might read an explanation text and why?

How to . . . indicates
instructions or advice

## How to build a pyramid . . . (with the help of 80,000 friends)

Numbered
points

Imperative
verbs at
beginning of
sentences

1   Clear the desert sand to show bare rock.
2   Level the site – perhaps allow water from the Nile to flood the base to give you a level.
3   Use the Pole Star to decide exactly where the north is.
4   Make a perfect square for the base and mark the four walls to face north, south, east and west.
5   Starting in the middle, build the first level with limestone blocks of 2 to 3 tons.
6   Add new levels, each one smaller than the one below. As the levels rise, build ramps of earth to slide the building blocks up.

Illustration

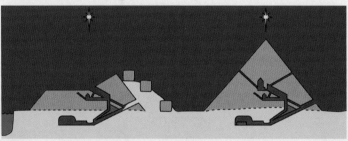

Second
person

7   As you build, don't forget to leave passageways and the central burial chamber. That burial chamber must end up directly beneath the point of the pyramid.
8   Cover the finished pyramid with the best Tura limestone and smooth it off.

Step-by-step
instructions
in sequenced
order

9   Remove the earth ramps and build a raised stone causeway from the river to the pyramid.
10  Wait of the Pharaoh to die. Mummify him. Bury him in the pyramid with his treasures. And don't forget to seal the pyramid to keep out robbers.

Short,
clear
sentences

# TASK

Read the text 'How to build a pyramid' and answer the following questions.
❶  What makes this text different from the first two texts?
❷  Can you think of three situations in which a set of instructions would be useful?

# The curse of the mummy's tomb

Dates and places to root text in real place/time

Suggestion of fact? or fiction?

## A true story?

### 26 November 1992

The great archaeologist, Howard Carter, had searched for years for a Pharaoh's tomb that hadn't been robbed. The pyramids were empty; the treasures stolen hundreds of years before. But there was still hope that the caves in the Valley of the Kings might have kept their secrets.

Paragraphs used to mark a change of focus/time/place

Connectives provide sign posts for the reader

At last he arrived at the entrance to an unbroken burial chamber. He called in the organiser of the expedition, Lord Carnarvon, to witness the final breakthrough. Carter described it as follows:

Events organised in chronological order

Third person

*With trembling hands I made a tiny hole in the upper left hand corner. Darkness and empty space, as far as an iron testing-rod could reach, showed that whatever lay beyond was empty. Widening the hole a little, I put in a candle and peered in. At first I could see nothing. The hot air escaping from the chamber caused the candle to flicker a little. But as my eyes became accustomed to the light, details of the room within emerged slowly from the mist; strange animals, statues and gold – everywhrere the glint of gold. I was struck dumb with amazement. Lord Carnarvon asked anxiously, "Can you see anything?" It was all I could do to get out the words, "Yes, wonderful things."*

First person

Active voice makes reader feel involved

Varied sentence structures

Painting a picture with words involves adjectives/adverbs/powerful verbs

Past tense

Dialogue used to forward plot

# TASK

Read the text 'The curse of the mummy's tomb' and answer the following questions.

❶ What do you notice about the style of the first two paragraphs and the style of the third? How do you account for this difference?

❷ Think of a recount text that might use:
- ❑ The first person
- ❑ The third person

# Text types recap

**Information texts** provide information. They are written for a reader who is interested and wants to find out more about the topic. Typical language features:

- Headings and sub-headings
- Tables and diagrams
- Third person
- Present tense
- Clear sentences – often simple or compound
- Connectives linked to sequence, cause and effect or comparison
- Facts and figures
- Some technical terms which may be explained in a glossary

**Explanation texts** explain how; they deal with processes. They often answer a question which begins with 'Why?' or 'How?'. Typical language features:

- Ideas clearly sequenced
- Paragraphs, bullet points or diagrams
- Third person
- A combination of past and present tense
- Mostly active voice
- Connectives linked to sequence, cause and effect or comparison
- Impersonal tone
- Some technical vocabulary
- Plain word choices

**Instruction texts** tell how something is done. There is an expectation that the reader will act upon the instructions. Typical language features:

- Clear, sequenced steps
- Easy to follow layout
- Short simple sentences
- Ideas organised chronologically, possibly in the form of a list
- Imperative verbs
- Present tense
- Implied second person
- Plain vocabulary

**Recount texts** retell a series of events. Typical language features:

- Ideas organised chronologically, usually in paragraphs
- First or third person
- Past tense
- Active voice
- Varied sentence structures
- Connectives linked to time
- Dates and places
- Adjectives and adverbs

# Charting text types

## TASK

Look again at the four different texts on pages 4–7. Using your knowledge of the specific language features for each text type, copy and complete the chart below.

| Text type | Title | Purpose | Structure and layout | Style and language features |
|---|---|---|---|---|
| Information | | | | |
| Recount | | | | |
| Explanation | | | | |
| Instructions | | | | |

## Planning and designing your ride

Now that you have revised the four non-fiction text types, you can begin to work on your ride designs for Terror Town. However, first you will find it helpful to look at the way some of the rides are described at a famous theme park. The rides are called Air, Nemesis, Oblivion and Submission.

With a partner, discuss these four names. What does each one suggest to you?

**Air** will give you the opportunity to fly, lying face down, soaring high above the ground then swooping down, your face inches from the ground! At dizzying speeds of 70 km per hour, this multi-million pound ride will give you the freedom to experience a flight of fancy like no other.

**Nemesis** pushes the senses to the limit – expect to experience G-forces of 4, (a space shuttle only hits 3G at take off), as well as four seconds of total weightlessness. Reaching speeds of up to 80 km per hour, Nemesis is definitely not for the faint-hearted.

**Oblivion** defies the limits of thrill ride technology to achieve a world first for a white knuckle ride: the face-first vertical drop rollercoaster. Held dangling 'on the edge' for three seconds, thrill seekers are faced with a terrifying 60 m drop into darkness, reaching speeds of 110 km per hour, with a maximum G-force of 4.5 – a physical and psychological challenge to experience.

Surrender yourself to **Submission**, which subjects its victims to 90 seconds of relentless spinning and inversion – counter rotating 15 m above ground level! This double inverted ride pounds the pulse and plunges the senses into freefall… so hang in there!

Work with a partner to identify:
- What happens on each ride
- What makes each ride original
- Why each ride would appeal to visitors

# TASK

❶ Work in groups of four or five to brainstorm ideas for the new Egyptian ride at Terror Town. Remember that the ride must be new and terrifying. What is your ride called and what makes it original?

❷ Using a large sheet of paper, map out your design.

❸ You should consider:
- ❑ A name for the ride
- ❑ What the ride would look like (sketch a picture of it)
- ❑ A description of what happens on the ride
- ❑ What makes it original
- ❑ Who it would appeal to and why

❹ As a team of designers you will be expected to present your ideas. The rest of the class will be the shareholders of Terror Town. You must take them through your design and be prepared to answer any questions they may have.

# TASK

Now you have finalised your design, the shareholders of Terror Town are keen to see it. A meeting has been called at which you are required to give a brief presentation, informing the shareholders about the new design and explaining why it will be popular. Your group has nominated you as its spokesperson!

❶ Use a copy of the following planning frame to prepare your presentation:

| Length of presentation: 10 minutes | Audience: Terror Town shareholders |
| --- | --- |
| Aim: to inform and explain | |
| Tone: formal; not colloquial or chatty. Use Standard English. | |
| How to begin… | |
| Five main points to make:<br><br>• <br>• <br>• <br>• <br>• | |
| How to conclude… | |

❷ You have been given the following advice which you should read before you give your presentation. With a partner, decide on the three most helpful tips.
   - ❏ Don't move about while you speak
   - ❏ Speak loudly and clearly
   - ❏ Vary your expression
   - ❏ Pause after an important point
   - ❏ Use appropriate hand gestures
   - ❏ Establish eye contact with your audience
   - ❏ Don't read from your notes
   - ❏ Don't mumble

❸ Deliver your presentation to the class.

Your presentation went well but unfortunately several shareholders were unable to attend. You must write a brief account for them, explaining your choice of design, saying why it will appeal to visitors and why you are sure it will be a success.

❶ Before you begin, look back at the Explanation texts box on page 8 and briefly revise its main features. The notes you made for your presentation will also help you.

❷ Use the sentence starters below to help you shape your writing.

- The new ride at Terror Town Theme Park is …
- It starts by …
- This means that …
- After that …
- Finally …
- The ride is unique in that …
- It will be extremely popular because …

## Press release

Now that your design for the new Egyptian ride has been accepted, it is time to inform the public. Terror Town Theme Park has decided to issue a press release and has asked you to write it.

# TASK

❶ Write a press release that describes your ride as precisely as possible.

❷ Before you begin, look back at the Information texts box on page 8 and briefly revise its main features.

❸ Now read the following press release. With a partner, make a note of:
- ❑ Its purpose and audience
- ❑ How far it follows the language features of an information text
- ❑ Its effectiveness

---

### PRESS RELEASE 26 February 2001

## TV stars bring characters to Lincolnshire Theme Park

With only days to go before the start of the 2001 season on 3 March at The Magical World of Fantasy Island at Ingoldmells on the Lincolnshire Coast, comes the news that the award-winning attraction has signed an exclusive deal. This will bring The Magic of Fantasy alive more than ever this year for kids with a plethora of children's favourite television characters appearing in live shows and meeting their young fans at the park. The deal with the Just Group PLC brings the latest children's TV stars the Butt Ugly Martians from children's ITV to the family visitor attraction.

Children will be entertained by the three alien heroes from the series. They are the advance force of the Martians that will be invading the themed resort at Easter and establishing an Earth base in Zaps Arcade at Fantasy Island.

The children's favourite television characters are not the only new additions for this season: the Park have invested £1.5 million pounds in a custom designed white knuckle terror-ride – 'The Beast' – with the warning that thrill seekers should beware, when it opens at Easter. A further attraction for members of the family is 'Tracker' with real scale vehicles including a yellow Cadillac that they can drive around a purpose built roadway.

**Fantasy Island opens for the 2001 season on 3 March (weekends only until 29 April).**
**Daily throughout the Easter holidays 13 April to 22 April.**
**Daily 5th May to 28 October.**

---

The points below will help you to plan your work.

**Six essential tips for writing a press release**

1. Tell your reader *why* they should read your press release.
2. Start with a *brief* description of the news.
3. Make sure the first ten words of your release are really effective.
4. Keep your writing simple and clear.
5. Deal with the facts.
6. Provide contact information: phone, fax, e-mail, website address.

❹ Now write your press release. When you have finished, share your work with a partner and comment on its effectiveness.

# Safety instructions

## TASK

The manager of Terror Town alerts you to the fact that you have not yet produced a set of safety instructions for your new ride. The ride opens tomorrow so it is vital that these are written immediately.

❶ Look back at the Instruction texts box on page 8 and briefly revise its main features.

❷ Work in groups to brainstorm any safety instructions which must apply to this ride. Now prune them so that you are left with five or six which you consider to be the most important. Remember that if instructions are too long or detailed, they are unlikely to be followed.

❸ Write your set of instructions, using:
- ❏ Numbers or bullet points
- ❏ Short, simple sentences
- ❏ Verbs in the imperative
- ❏ Present tense
- ❏ Clear vocabulary

❹ Present your instructions clearly for class display.

# News report

On the day it opens, the terrifying new ride at Terror Town makes it into the local news. You are going to write a short news report.

❶ Before you begin, read the following newspaper report about plans for a new Youth Council in Woking. Newspaper reports are sometimes known as media recounts, whereas first person recounts such as autobiographies are usually known as personal recounts. Although the first paragraph of a media recount often gives the most important points straight away, the rest of the report normally uses the chronological structure you would expect of a recount text.

❷ Look back at the features of a recount on page 8 and consider how far this newspaper report uses the same language features.

❸ Finally, write your own short news report. You should remember to:
- Think of an attention grabbing headline
- Use a sub-headline
- Include a lead paragraph which answers the questions who, what, where and when
- Write in short paragraphs
- Include quotations from people involved

## 'Run by young people for young people'

### If approved, nominations will be needed for Youth Council

TEENAGE power will soon come into play after a Youth Council for Woking borough got the go-ahead on October 3.

The proposal now has to be agreed at full council on October 17.

The idea of a forum for young people was given fresh impetus following a motion tabled by Cllr James Palmer calling for the formation of a Youth Council as a way of involving teenagers in local decision making.

He said: "I am delighted that the idea of the Youth Council received cross party support at the executive.

"The purpose of the Youth Council will be fourfold – to better inform Woking Borough Council in its decision making processes; to work up projects to meet identified needs in the borough; to engage young people in the community; and to help develop the citizenship skills of young people."

Following consultation with young people across Woking, it is proposed the Youth Council will consist of up to 24 members aged between 11 to 18 who either live, work or study in Woking.

**Support**
It would also receive support from Woking council officers and have a budget of £10,000 to spend on projects for young people (subject to basic financial safeguards).

Cllr Palmer added: "The Youth Council is to be run by young people. This is a real opportunity to get involved and make a difference."

## Working on your own – producing a publicity leaflet

Your project is now complete and it has been an enormous success. The new Egyptian ride at Terror Town is the most popular ride there. Over 10,000 visitors a day are expected to have the fright of their lives on your ride!

## Working on your own

Your final task in this unit is to produce a leaflet about the new ride for visitors to Terror Town. To complete the leaflet you will need to use a variety of text types. You must organise the leaflet in a way that is appropriate for its audience and purpose.

Your leaflet should include the following:

● Information about the ride
● An explanation of how the ride works
● Instructions for safety on the ride
● A first-hand report of a visitor's experience of the ride

Your leaflet should aim to tell the visitor as much as possible about the ride in as short a space as possible. They will need to read the leaflet as they walk around the theme park. Think carefully about methods of presentation which will make it accessible and easy to follow. Remember that the theme park attracts many children and young people and your leaflet must appeal to them too!

## TASK

Work with a partner to review your learning.

❶ Make a note of the three most important things you have learnt in this unit.

❷ Many of these non-fiction text types are used in subjects other than English. Can you think of other subjects which expect you to read and write:
- ❏ A recount text?
- ❏ Instructions?
- ❏ An information text?
- ❏ An explanation text?
- ❏ A mixture of more than one of the above?

❸ Note down three ways in which you will be able to apply what you have learnt to other subject areas.

# UNIT 2

## The Star Beast

In this unit you will learn about the following key objectives by learning how to:

**Draft** – find the best ingredients for your own story; the right words, sentences and ideas so that you can engross your reader

**Structure a story** – re-draft and polish your story so that it is the best you can produce

**Infer and deduce** – make educated guesses about meanings from the story so that you can transfer these skills to your own writing

**Start paragraphs** – recognise cues to new paragraphs and vary the way you use your own paragraphs

**Consider word meaning in context** – define and deploy words with precision so that they have real impact on your reader

You will be asked to read a story, understand how it is put together and think carefully about what it means and how you will use these ideas to plan your own piece of narrative writing. As you move through the unit, you will keep a 'Writing Jotter'. Most writers keep a notebook of this kind where they jot down ideas, details or snippets of powerful language to use in their own writing. Your jotter will gradually build into plans, detailed sections and, finally, into the writing of your extended narrative.

It is time to think about what makes a story. What are the basic elements that we all know from childhood? As you develop your understanding of the structure of a story, you will be asked to contribute to a class display highlighting the key elements.

Another way in which you can become a really effective writer is to talk about your work. To help with this, you will be asked to set up your own 'Writer's Forum' – a group of supportive peers who will act as your friendly critics.

## TASK

❶ Working with a partner, think of as many story elements as you can, e.g. three wishes, an ugly sister, a dark wood.

# The story bag

You are going to explore the world of stories. Stories are common to all cultures across the world and many of them have similar features, characters and events.

As experienced readers yourselves, you will have a vast repertoire of characters, incidents and language forms which combine to make stories. You will have learnt many of these from your early childhood, and all of us share this heritage.

This investigation of stories asks you to explore the 'Story bag' collage and identify the familiar characters, ideas, settings and themes which form the bedrock of most stories.

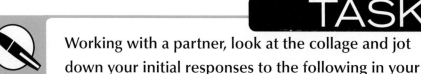

## TASK

Working with a partner, look at the collage and jot down your initial responses to the following in your writing jotter:

❶ Choose three story elements from the collage.
❷ How do you react to them as a reader? What do they suggest to you?
❸ What often happens when these elements are included in stories?
❹ Write a few lines from a story you make up together which includes these three elements. Work in a small group.

You will often be working in small groups during this unit because talking about your writing is a powerful way to improve.

# TASK

❶ Now, discuss your ideas, suggestions and insights
with the rest of the class in the Writer's Forum.

❷ Share your ideas and your thinking about stories
with the class.

# Starting stories

Look at the way this story begins and read the annotations to get you thinking about how you might start a story.

A storm often suggests that trouble is coming in a story

'The wind howled around Brimstone Mansion as the carriage carrying young Lady Derbyshire drew up at the imposing front gate. It opened slowly, with a grinding creak yet no-one appeared to be in attendance…'

The main character is often young, alone and vulnerable in a ghost story

A story which starts like this is likely to be a ghost story. Can you see why?

## TASK

You are about to begin writing your own story. To help you do this, you will be reading a parallel story, which will act as a model for your own writing. The short story is called, 'The Star Beast' and the writer is Nicholas Stuart Gray.

❶ Before you begin reading, focus on the title. Predict what you think might happen in the story. Make a short entry in your jotter. It might say something like:

> 'I think that this story is going to be about a creature that is just the very best at everything it does. It's a sort of David Beckham of the jungle.'

❷ Now, begin reading 'The Star Beast'.

## The Star Beast

Soon upon a time, and not so far ahead, there was a long streak of fire, and a terrible bang that startled all who heard it, even those who were inured to such noise. When day came the matter was discussed, argued and finally dismissed. For no one could discover any cause at all for the disturbance.

Shortly afterwards, at a farm, there was heard a scrabbling at the door, and a crying. When the people went to see what was there, they found a creature. It was not easy to tell what sort of creature it was but far too easy to tell that it was hurt and hungry and afraid. Only its pain and hunger had brought it to the door for help.

# TASK

❶ Now, in your groups, begin your own stories. Remember, you can use the ideas from the collage and the story 'The Star Beast', or your own ideas. As a writer at this early stage, you will want to write only short sections and keep thinking about what you are doing and why. So, keep it to 50 words and use your jotter to reflect on your progress.

❷ Next, work with a partner and read your work aloud to each other. As readers/listeners, see if you can spot ways in which you have been 'hooked'. Give your supportive response to your partner's work.

❸ Share some interesting openings with the rest of the group and discuss why they work so well. As a class, choose the best story openings for a class display on 'narrative structure'.

# Which way and why?

Now that you have some idea of how your story starts and the language style that you will be using, it is time to consider the possibilities for your story. Many stories follow a common structure but have their own individual twists and turns. It is up to you, as the writer, to make these decisions now so that you guide your reader and shape the responses. This section deals with 'tension'. Tension is the excitement or emotion which builds up in a story.

## TASK

❶ Look at the illustration on the opposite page. It maps the tension levels in Little Red Riding Hood. Choose a different story and decide on the levels of tension at each point. Try mapping out the tension in Snow White, if you need a suggestion.

❷ Many stories share common elements and you have already uncovered some of them in the collage exercise completed earlier. This next task will help you to explore how stories are put together like the building blocks of a house. Read through the 'Route map' for stories. In your jotters, write down responses to the following questions:

❑ When is the tension at its peak in this story?

❑ Why do you think this is so?

❑ What other sort of events might occur in the crisis?

❑ How do stories resolve themselves?

❑ What sort of ending might you consider for your story? Why?

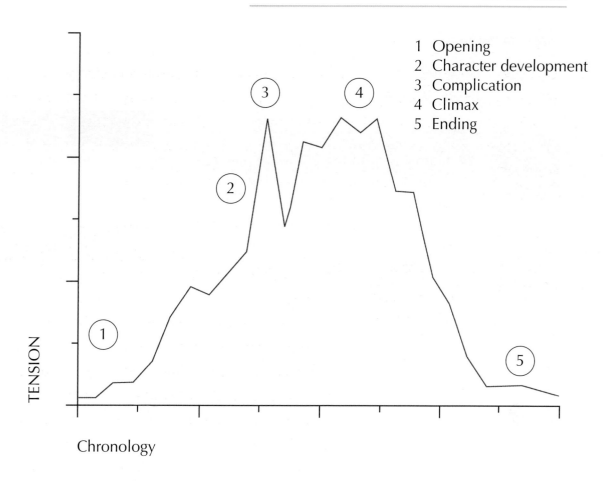

1  Opening
2  Character development
3  Complication
4  Climax
5  Ending

TENSION

Chronology

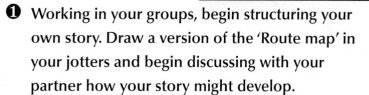

## TASK

❶ Working in your groups, begin structuring your own story. Draw a version of the 'Route map' in your jotters and begin discussing with your partner how your story might develop.

❷ Feed your ideas back to all the other groups.

# The stepping stones of happenings

A 'plot' in a story refers to the events – the stepping stones of happenings – which keep the reader interested as the story moves on.

❶ Skim and scan the following passage for more evidence of the attitudes of the farmer and his wife towards the creature in their care and what it might mean in the plot.

❷ What are the stepping stones of the plot in this short section of 'The Star Beast'?

Use your jotter to record them.

Being used to beasts, the farmer and his wife tended the thing. They put it in a loose-box and tended it. They brought water in a big basin and it drank thirstily, but with some difficulty – for it seemed to want to lift it to its mouth instead of lapping, and the big basin was too big, and it was too weak. So it lapped. The farmer dressed the great burn that seared its thigh and shoulder and arm. He was kind enough, in a rough way, but the creature moaned, and set its teeth, and muttered strange sounds, and clenched its front paws….

   Those front paws…! They were so like human hands that it was quite startling to see them. Even with their soft covering of grey fur they were slender, long-fingered, with the fine nails of a girl. And its body was like that of a boy – a half grown lad – though it was tall as a man. Its head was man-shaped. The long and slanting eyes were as yellow as topaz, and shone from inside with their own light. And the lashes were thick and silvery.

## TASK

❶ Working in pairs, begin to plan how to develop a character for your story. What are the characteristics/features of your character? What effect does it have on you as a reader? Copy your ideas in your jotter and be ready to share them with the rest of the group.

❷ Begin your short presentation to the rest of the class. You might like to start off with:

   'My plot will be developed by a character which…'

❸ Your next task is to be researchers of stories. Explore stories you find on the web, in your school library or at home. What are the classic ways in which stories use characters to engage the interest of the reader? Bring the results of your research to class. You might want to work in pairs on this.

# TASK

When we read, it is possible to respond in two very different ways. Denotation is a very literal and simple response to a text. For instance, if we read about a 'tree', it might denote, 'a plant made from wood usually with leaves'. However, the same tree might suggest different things to a reader. For instance, the 'tree' might suggest 'nature' or 'growth'. This wider response would be a connotation of the word 'tree'.

❶ Look back over the story so far. In pairs, choose two key words which interest you. What do these words denote to you? What connotations (wider responses) do they suggest to you?

❷ Now, read the next instalment of our story, 'The Star Beast'. As you read, look out for moments in the text when you use denotation and connotation. Record two examples in your jotter.

'It's a monkey of some kind,' decided the farmer.

'But so beautiful,' said his wife. 'I've never heard of a monkey like this. They're charming – pretty – amusing – all in their own way. But not as beautiful as a real person might be.' They were concerned when the creature refused to eat. It turned away its furry face, with those wonderful eyes, the straight nose, and curving fine lips, and would not touch the best of the season's hay. It would not touch the dog biscuits or the bones. Even the boiled cod-head that was meant for the cat's supper, it refused. In the end, it settled for milk. It lapped it delicately out of the big basin, making small movements of its hands – its forepaws – as though it would have preferred some smaller utensil that it could lift to its mouth.

Word went round. People came to look at the strange and injured creature in the barn. Many people came. From the village, the town, and the city. They prodded it, and examined it, turning it this way and that. But no one could decide just what it was. A beast for sure. A monkey, most likely. Escaped from a circus or menagerie. Yet whoever had lost it made no attempt to retrieve it, made no offer of reward for its return.

Its injuries healed. The soft fur grew again over the bare grey skin. Experts from the city came and took it away for more detailed examination.'

# TASK

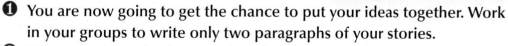

❶ You are now going to get the chance to put your ideas together. Work in your groups to write only two paragraphs of your stories.

❷ When you have finished, work with a response partner. Read your paragraphs aloud and ask your partner how he or she responded. Were there times when you responded using denotation and connotation? Explain these occasions to each other.

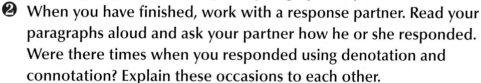

❸ If you are brave, volunteer to demonstrate your work as response partners in pairs in front of the whole class.

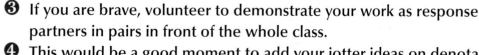

❹ This would be a good moment to add your jotter ideas on denotation and connotation to the wall display.

## Main and minor characters

You are now going to use some drama strategies to explore the relationships between the main character, the Star Beast, and the minor characters. When you have done this, you will be asked to develop your own main/minor characters in your stories with a clear relationship between them.

## Tableaux and text

### What is a tableau?

A tableau is a dramatic technique for exploring in depth the relationships between characters in stories. When you do this you will need to think carefully about how your body language, gestures and facial expressions convey your understanding of the meaning in the text.

As an example, read this extract, then analyse the way the pupils in the picture have interpreted the relationships between the characters:

> The wife of the farmer was sad to see it go. She had grown quite attached to it.
> 'It was getting to know me,' said she. 'And it talked to me – in its fashion.'
> The farmer nodded slowly and thoughtfully.
> 'It was odd,' he said, 'the way it would imitate what one said. You know, like a parrot does. Not real talking, of course, just imitation.'
> 'Of course,' said his wife. 'I never thought it was real talk. I'm not so silly.'
> It was good at imitating speech, the creature.

Read on and, as you do so, try to find suitable moments in the text when you might be able to use tableaux again to explore the relationships between the characters.

Very soon, it had learned many words and phrases, and began to string them together quite quickly, and with surprising sense. One might have thought it knew what it meant – if one was silly.

The professors and elders and priests who now took the creature in hand were far from silly. They were puzzled, and amused, and interested – at first. They looked at it, in the disused monkey-cage at the city's menagerie, where it was kept. And it stood upright, on finely-furred feet as arched and perfect as the feet of an ancient statue.

'It is oddly human,' said the learned man.

They amused themselves by bringing it a chair and watching it sit down gracefully, though not very comfortably, as if it was used to furniture of better shape and construction. They gave it a plate and a cup, and it ate with its hands most daintily, looking round as though for some sort of cutlery. But it was not thought safe to trust it with a knife.

'It is only a beast,' said everyone. 'However clever at imitation.'

'It's so quick to learn,' said some.

'But not in any way human.'

'No,' said the creature, 'I am not human. But, in my own place, I am a man.'

'Parrot-talk!' laughed the elders, uneasily.

The professors of living and dead languages taught it simple speech.

After a week, it said to them;

'I understand all the words you use. They are very easy. And you cannot quite express what you mean, in any of your tongues. A child of my race ---' It stopped, for it had no wish to seem impolite, and then it said, 'There is a language that is spoken throughout the universe. If you will allow me ----'

# TASK

❶ Now that you have read this section of the story try using tableaux yourself to explore the relationship between the farmer and his wife and the Star Beast. Find some crucial lines of text to use as narration for your tableau to give it time, place and significance.

❷ What do your tableaux reveal about the relationship between the Star Beast and others?

❸ Move into your writing groups and begin to shape your own main and minor characters by placing them in a tableau and closely examining it. What does it reveal about their relationships?

❹ Quickly repeat your tableaux but, this time, explain the relationships to your class.

# Inference and deduction

## TASK

❶ Quickly scan through the story so far and locate five words which you feel you still have not quite learnt. Write them on your whiteboards. Now working in pairs, use the 'Look, Cover, Say, Write, Check' method in your jotters and see if you have learnt them.

❷ Get your partner to test you.

❸ Talk to your partner about what has happened so far in the story.

❹ Now, working in your groups, use this next section of 'The Star Beast' to do your own detective work. Work in pairs and make your own inferences and deductions in your jotters. What can you infer and deduce about: the crowd; the beast; the way the author wants you to respond as a reader?

---

And softly and musically it began to utter a babble of meaningless nonsense at which all the professors laughed loudly.

'Parrot-talk!' they jeered. 'Pretty Polly! Pretty Polly!'

For they were much annoyed. And they mocked the creature into cowering silence.

The professors of logic came to the same conclusions as the others.

'Your logic is at fault,' the creature had told them, despairingly. 'I have disproved your conclusions again and again. You will not listen or try to understand.'

'Who could not understand parrot-talk?'

'I am no parrot, but a man in my own place. Define a man. I walk upright. I think. I speak. What is a man by your definition?'

'Pretty Polly!' said the professors.

They were very angry. One of them hit the creature with his walking-cane. No one liked to be set on a level with a beast. And the beast covered its face with its hands, and was silent.

*Deduction* using reasoning move from the general to the particular

*Inference*: arrive at a logical conclusion

## TASK

❶ Working in pairs, test each other verbally on one spelling from earlier.

❷ Then, read out to the class one example from today's story extract when you inferred or deduced from the text. Ask the class to listen to your example and then ask how your listeners inferred or deduced from the same piece of text.

❸ Use post-it notes to place these comments on the display.

## Purple paragraph starters

Finding ways to intrigue your reader by varying the way you start paragraphs and connect ideas is an interesting writing exercise.

# TASK

Now, read on and, as you do, look for interesting ways in which paragraph links have been made. Write down two examples in your jotter.

---

It was warier when the mathematicians came. It added two and two together for them. They were amazed. It subtracted eight from ten. They wondered at it. It divided twenty by five. They marvelled. It took courage. It said:

'But you have reached a point where your formulae and calculuses fail. There is a simple law – one by which you reached the earth long ago – one by which you can leave it at will ----'

The professors were furious.

'Parrot! Parrot!' they shouted

'No! In my own place -----'

The beast fell silent.

Then came the priests, smiling kindly – except to one another. For with each other they argued furiously and loathingly regarding their own views on rule and theory.

'Oh stop!' said the creature, pleadingly.

It lifted its hands towards them and its golden eyes were full of pity.

'You make everything petty and meaningless,' it said. 'Let me tell you of the Master-Plan of the Universe. It is so simple and nothing to do with fear.'

---

# TASK

❶ Try out some different paragraph starters and connectives in your own stories. Return to your writing groups to review your story so far. At each paragraph break, think of three new ways of grabbing your reader's attention by varying the connective or technique you have seen used earlier. Work in pairs and don't forget to use your jotter to explain your thinking.

❷ Re-convene the Writer's Forum. Read out your ideas on paragraph connectives, explain your reasoning and listen to the response of your classmates.

❸ Return to your stories. Spend some time re-drafting and thinking of ways to sharpen your links and ideas so that there is maximum impact on your reader. You could add some suggestions to the display at this point.

## Narrative devices

A narrative device is a kind of trick writers use to keep their readers guessing or interested (readers easily get bored!). To begin this section, you will look briefly at spelling and then at a variety of narrative devices used in 'The Star Beast'. You now have a chance to put some narrative devices into your story before you share your ideas with the rest of the class in the Writer's Forum.

## TASK

In your groups, look closely at the next section from 'The Star Beast', particularly at the sections in bold. Read these sections aloud and decide on one reason why each of these narrative devices is effective. Two examples have been done for you. Put your reasons into your jotter.

---

**The one word of dialogue and the exclamation mark gives the word real force**

**A short sentence can add real impact to your writing. This sentence really emphasises the hate the elders felt because it is so stark and direct**

'The priests were so outraged that they forgot to hate one another. They screamed wildly **with one voice.**
► **'Wicked!'**
They fled from the creature, jamming in the cage door in their haste to escape and forgot the soul-less evil thing. And the beast sighed and hid its sorrowful face, and took refuge in increasing silence.
► **The elders grew to hate it.** They disliked the imitating and the parrot-talk, the golden eyes, the sorrow, the pity. **They took away its chair, its table, its plate and cup (1).** They ordered it to walk properly – on all fours, like any other beast.
   **'But in my own place ---- (2)'**
It broke off there. Yet some sort of pride, or stubbornness, or courage, made it refuse to crawl, no matter what they threatened or did.
   **They sold it to a circus (3).'**

**'One voice'** suggests that all the priests agreed with each other. It emphasised how alone the Star Beast is

---

## TASK

❶ In your writing groups, look closely at what you have written so far. Locate moments in your story where you feel it might be necessary or interesting to add a particular narrative device. Which one should it be? Why? Don't forget to use your jotter to record your reasons.

❷ Re-convene the Writer's Forum and share your ideas on narrative devices by reading one aloud to the group, explaining your reasoning and asking for comments.

❸ Add to your display.

# Using words with precision

Being very, very careful about the words you use as a writer can have a real impact on your reader. This section is designed to help you become discerning in your use of words.

*Discerning*: having a true insight into the meaning; to have acute judgement

## TASK

As you read on, notice the way in which Nicholas Stuart Gray, the writer, uses words precisely to elicit a particular response from us as readers. When you come to the vocabulary in bold, stop for a moment. Below, there are alternative words which might have been used by the writer. Would you use the alternative words? Why? Explain your reasons in your jotter.

*it*

A small sum was sent to the farmer who had first found **the thing**, and the rest of its price went into the state coffers for making weapons for a pending war.

as some men are

The man who owned the circus was not especially brutal, **as such men go**. He was used to training beasts, for he was himself the chief attraction of the show, with his lions and tigers,

dozy

**half-drugged** and toothless as they were. He said it was no use being too easy on animals.

'They don't understand over-kindness,' said he. ' They get to **despising** you. You have to show who's master.'

hating

He showed the creature who was master. He made it jump through hoops and do simple sums on a blackboard. At first it also tried to speak to the people who came to look at it. It would say, in its soft and bell-clear tones:

'Oh, listen – I can tell you things ---'

## TASK

❶ In your writing groups, swap your work with a partner. Skim each other's stories for five possible words which might be improved.

❷ Use a dictionary or thesaurus to find alternative words. Choose the best and explain your reasons to each other.

❸ Present your 'best' words to the Writer's Forum with your reasons.

Everyone was amazed at its cleverness and most entertained by the eager way it spoke. And such parrot-nonsense it talked!

'Hark at it!' they cried. 'It wants to tell us things, bless it!'

'About the other side of the moon!'

'The far side of saturn!'

'Who taught it to say all this stuff?'

'It's saying something about the block in mathematics now!'

'And the language of infinity!'

'Logic!'

'And the Master-Plan!'

They rolled about, helpless with laughter in their ringside seats.

It was even more entertaining to watch the creature doing its sums on the big black-board, which two attendants would turn so that everyone could admire the cleverness: 2 and 2, and the beautifully-formed 4 that it wrote beneath. $10 - 8 = 2$. 5 into $20 - 11$ from 12.

'How clever it is,' said a small girl admiringly.

Her father smiled.

'It's the trainer who's clever,' he said. 'The animal knows nothing of what it does. Only what it has been taught. By kindness, of course,' he added quickly, as the child looked sad.

'Oh good,' said she, brightening. 'I wouldn't like it hurt. It's so sweet.'

But even she had to laugh when it came to the hoop-jumping. For the creature hated doing it, and, although the long whip of the trainer never actually touched its grey fur, yet it cowered at the cracking sound. Surprisingly, if anyone had wondered why. And it ran, upright on its fine furred feet, and graceful in spite of the red and yellow clothes it was wearing, and it jumped through the hoops. And then more hoops were brought. And these were surrounded by inflammable material and set on fire. The audience was enthralled. For the beast was terrified of fire, for some reason. It would shrink back and clutch at its shoulder, its arm, its thigh. It would stare up wildly into the roof of the great circus canopy – as if it could see through it and out to the sky beyond – as though it sought desperately for help that would not come.

And it shook and trembled. And the whip cracked. And it cried aloud as it came to each flaming hoop. But it jumped.

# TASK

**❶** In your writing groups, work in pairs. You are going to help each other to use words more exactly in your writing. Decide whose writing you will look at first.

**❷** Read through the writing and find five examples of words which you think you might use to have more impact; more bite; words which need to be used more precisely. When you have found five examples, use a dictionary or a thesaurus and find at least two synonyms.

**❸** Discuss between you which of these words would be best for your story. Are you looking for more power, sympathy, shock value? What are your reasons? When you have finished, swap writing and find five words in your partner's writing and repeat the activity.

**❹** In the Writer's Forum, present your decisions on your choice of words to the group. Choose your two most powerful examples and explain your reasons.

*Synonym*: a word that has the same meaning as another word

*Thesaurus*: a treasure house. Usually used to describe a book which provides a vast number of words, quotations etc.

# Crisis? What crisis?

Traditionally in stories, there is nearly always a moment (referred to as the crisis) around which the whole story turns. It is the moment of decision or the moment when the characters' lives are changed forever by a particular event. We are going to explore the notion of a 'crisis'.

> *Crisis*: **a significant point in time; a turning point**

And it stopped talking to the people. Sometimes it would almost speak, but then it would give a hunted glance towards the ring master, and lapse into silence. Yet always it walked and ran and jumped as a man would do these things – upright. Not on all fours, like a proper beast.

And soon a particularly dangerous tightrope dance took the fancy of the people. The beast was sold to a small touring animal-show. It was getting very poor in entertainment value, anyway. It moved sluggishly. Its fur was draggled and dull. It had even stopped screaming at the fiery hoops. And – it was such an eerie, man-like thing to have around. Everyone was glad to see it go.

In the dreary little show where it went, no one even pretended to understand animals. They just showed them in their cages. Their small, fetid cages. To begin with, the keeper would bring the strange creature out to perform for the onlookers. But it was a boring performance. Whip or no whip, hunger or less hunger, the beast could no longer run or jump properly. It shambled round and round, dull eyed and silent. People merely wondered what sort of animal it was, but not with any great interest. It could hardly even be made to flinch at fire, not even when sparks touched its fur. It was sold to a collector of rare beasts. And he took it to his little menagerie on the edge of his estate near a forest.

He was not really very interested in his creatures. It was a passing hobby for a very rich man. Something to talk about among his friends. Only once he came to inspect his new acquisition. He prodded it with a stick. He thought it rather an ugly, dreary animal.

'I heard that you used to talk parrot-fashion,' said he. 'Go on, then, say something.'

It only cowered. He prodded it some more.

'I read about you when they had you in the city.' Said the man, prodding harder. 'You used to talk, I know you did, so talk now. You used to say all sorts of clever things. That you were a man in your own place. Go on, tell me you're a man.'

'Pretty Polly,' mumbled the creature, almost inaudibly.

Nothing would make it speak again.

It was so boring that no one took much notice or care of it. And one night it escaped from its cage.

# TASK

Read the extract opposite and answer the following questions.

❶ Discuss in pairs why you think the moment of escape for the Star Beast is a crisis.

❷ Working in your groups, plan a crisis within your story. What could it be? What will happen to change the characters' lives? Why will you give it this crisis? Discuss your ideas and then use your jotter to record them.

❸ In the Writer's Forum, share your moments of crisis. Invent a symbol/picture for your crisis and place it on the display.

❹ You are now going to be asked to take a hot seat as the writer of your story. Spend a few minutes discussing this and jot down your ideas. You will need to consider how you (the writer) might use language (body and verbal) to express yourself. As preparation before the next lesson, think of answers to the following questions:

❑ How would you describe your main character to us?

❑ Why did you create a character like that?

❑ What did you decide on for a crisis?

❑ Are you satisfied with your crisis?

❑ How could it have been made more dramatic?

❑ Have you decided on an ending?

❑ What are your reasons at the moment?

## All's well that ends well?

All stories need a powerful, poignant ending, something to really make the reader think. Perhaps it might be a shocking ending, something completely unexpected with a twist? Or, it might be the kind of ending which neatly solves all of the problems, possibly a 'happy ending'.

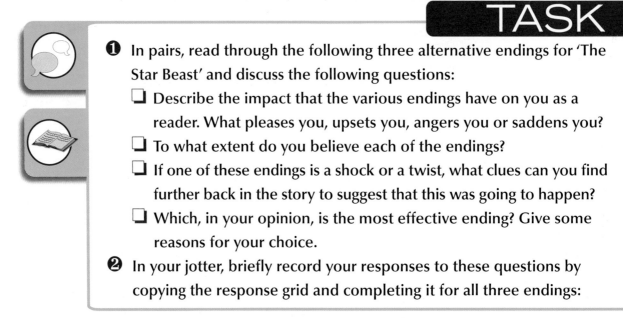

## TASK

❶ In pairs, read through the following three alternative endings for 'The Star Beast' and discuss the following questions:

❏ Describe the impact that the various endings have on you as a reader. What pleases you, upsets you, angers you or saddens you?

❏ To what extent do you believe each of the endings?

❏ If one of these endings is a shock or a twist, what clues can you find further back in the story to suggest that this was going to happen?

❏ Which, in your opinion, is the most effective ending? Give some reasons for your choice.

❷ In your jotter, briefly record your responses to these questions by copying the response grid and completing it for all three endings:

|  | Issues | Comments |
|---|---|---|
| Ending 1<br>Death of the Star Beast | Tragic ending<br>Believable<br>Inevitable<br>Very powerful | I didn't want this to happen<br>He couldn't do anything else<br>Everyone was against him<br>I was sad because he deserved better |
| Ending 2 |  |  |
| Ending 3 |  |  |

## Ending 1

The beast ran quickly – away from the circus; as far away and as quickly as it could possibly go. But the night mist began to fall and the moon disappeared behind a bank of dark clouds and it quickly lost its way. Soon, it was stumbling in the wilderness, unable to find shelter or food or comfort. For too long it had been starved and ridiculed and beaten and this…this being lost and alone was worse than everything before. The cold, the darkness and the awful solitude overwhelmed it and, when it came to the foot of a sombre oak, it laid itself on the wet earth to sleep for ever.

## Ending 2

> The last glimpse that anyone saw of it was by a hunter in the deeps of the forest.
>   It was going slowly looking in terror at rabbits and squirrels. It was weeping aloud and trying to desperately walk on all fours.

## Ending 3

> The beast ran quickly through the night, exhausted and hungry but determined never again to be treated as it had been. When it was almost at its wits end with tiredness, it glimpsed the light of a small cottage in the distance. Tentatively, it knocked on the old oak door and the grey haired elderly man who answered took pity and gave it shelter. Quite by chance, this old man was a professor...a professor of astronomy, and he knew of the existence of planets and beings and far off civilisations. As the days turned into weeks and the weeks into months, the professor and The Star Beast talked until their friendship was a bond of truth.
>   On the first day of the first month of the new year, the professor held a conference at the university. The star attraction was his friend and colleague and companion. And all that they now understood was acknowledged and shared and accepted by all.

# TASK

❶ When you have made your decisions about these endings, share your views with the rest of the group in the Writer's Forum. The actual ending which Nicholas Stuart Gray decided upon is number 2.

❷ It is time to write your own ending. Working in pairs within your groups, try writing for a few minutes and then share what you have written with your partner. Remember to work as response partners. What do you think works well for the reader? Does the ending make sense to the reader? Does it have impact on the reader?

❸ Be prepared to read your 'work in progress' during the Writer's Forum and to explain to others why, as a writer, you have made these choices.

# Writer's hot seat

Writers are real people who make real choices about their characters, plot, themes and settings. They try to influence readers by appealing to their emotions and by using words and sentences deliberately, with great care, to make an impression. This is your chance to find out why Nicholas Stuart Gray wrote 'The Star Beast' and, perhaps, to find out a little more about his decisions and choices as a writer.

1 Imagine that this writer was available to you now, in your classroom, and that you could ask him questions.

2 Find a partner and spend no more than three minutes thinking of three really thoughtful questions that you could put to him.

3 Now, either your teacher, or a volunteer from the group, is going to work in role by pretending to be Nicholas Stuart Gray in the hot seat. Arrange the room so that there is a chair facing the audience, as in the photograph below.

Be ready to volunteer to help out the 'writer' in case of any tricky questions. This would allow the person in the hot seat to have 'Time out' and quickly confer with the helper. When you are ready to begin, find someone to ask the first question and move into the hot seat. It is not just Nicholas Stuart Gray who is a writer in your group. Everyone is now a writer. So, everyone has made decisions about characters, plots, themes, settings and language choices. It should be possible for all of you to experience the hot seat as writers. An explanation of the process is given opposite.

# TASK

❹ Organise yourselves into pairs A and B. A will interview first; B will be interviewed as the writer.

❺ Prepare your questions in your jotter. You might want to use the 'Question support' section below.

**Question support:**
- What sort of story were you trying to create?
- Why do you feel that section of the story is so effective?
- Specifically, what problems did you encounter during the writing?
- Tell me about the characters. Which is your favourite creation and why?
- How did you try to grab your reader's attention?
- You had a number of types of ending to choose from. Why did you decide on this one?

❻ In pairs, use the hot seat technique. Decide who should go first. Try to really probe with your questioning – try to get to the bottom of the writer's decisions and choices about characters, plot, themes, settings and language choices, then swap roles.

❼ After the hot seat, use your jotters to briefly note down three key decisions you made about your story. Then think of two ways in which the hot seating helped you to think critically about your story.

❽ Finally, share some of your key decisions and insights from the hot seat with the rest of the group in the Writer's Forum.

❾ All stories need a reader who can respond to it. Find a reader from outside school who can read and respond to what you have written. You are going to use the responses of this reader to shape your final draft. Copy this next section onto a blank slip of paper and attach it to your story:

> **Reader's feedback:** Please read this story and give your supportive response in writing to the following key points in no more than 100 words – the impact of the story, your impressions of the characters, the impact of the ending.

## Readers and responses

A   What really impressed me most about this short story was the way the characters just leapt off the page. I could really see them in my mind's eye as the story began to unfold and I was completely caught up in their problems and dilemmas.

B   This story moved with real pace and action. It was a thrill a minute and I was on the edge of my seat the whole time. By the end, I was almost too exhausted to be able to take in the clever twist which resolved the problems and left me wanting to read more.

C   What a tear-jerker! This short story had everything. The tension built up until I could hardly bear to read on and then quite suddenly, it let me down very gently with a most satisfying ending.

D   Well, who would have thought it? A romantic love story combined with a science fiction thriller and it works! The meeting between the two central characters in the cargo hold of the space fleet was very cleverly developed and they become the central focus in a narrative which took me, as reader, on a journey through the stars.

E   I would never have thought of going where this story took me. It was full of twists, turns and surprises. From the moment it started, I was hooked. Great characters, loads of action, some very emotional moments and a thoughtful and surprising ending. I want to read it again!

## TASK

❶ Using a strip of blank paper, write down one comment from your reader which you would like to discuss publicly.
❷ Place the strip of paper on your group's almost completed display chart.
❸ Share your comment by reading it to the class and explaining why you have chosen it for the display.

The whole point of this unit has been to improve your writing. In order to achieve this, you have completed a variety of tasks and, hopefully, your narrative. However, this is only part of becoming a better writer. As well as completing the tasks, you have become more aware of yourself as a writer who understands how stories are constructed and who knows how to apply the conventions of narrative writing.

The best way to improve as a writer is to seek out an audience, as you did earlier, and brace yourself for more constructive criticism.

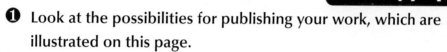

# TASK

 **❶** Look at the possibilities for publishing your work, which are illustrated on this page.

 **❷** Discuss in pairs which option you will take for your story.

**❸** In your jotters, write down the steps you will need to take in order to get your story published in this way. For example, if you can find a children's publisher listed on the internet in your school library, you could send your story through on e-mail!

 **❹** When you have decided, really commit yourself to it by making a declaration and posting it on the display. It could start like this...

'I (your name) am making a commitment to have my work published in .................. by (state a date).

Signed.......................'

## Talking to write

*Glossary*: a list of definitions or ideas connected to a common theme

## A glossary of strategies for improving writing during group work

When you are working on your planning, drafting and re-drafting as a writer, it is useful to have a supportive partner or group to give you feedback on your ideas. Here are a collection of strategies which might help.

| Strategy | Purpose |
|---|---|
| 1 Read a sentence aloud to your partner | This will give you immediate feedback on whether or not your sentence makes sense. |
| 2 Read around the group | Often useful for listening to the way others have tackled a description. It will give you plenty of ideas to use in your work. |
| 3 Check on a word | Asking for help with a particular word – how it is spelt, whether anyone can think of a better word, does the alliteration work? |
| 4 Check connectives with a partner | Useful when you want to get feedback on the flow of one paragraph into another. |
| 5 Dictionary hunt | Pause from your writing and find two or three words which you feel are not 'quite right'. Swap words with your partner and find synonyms or other alternatives. |
| 6 Jotter sharing | Use your jotters in pairs so that you take turns recording your impressions, insights and understanding. |
| 7 Writing swap | Swap your stories at similar points and draft the next paragraph for your partner. This might be a useful way to help generate new ideas. |
| 8 Getting out of a hole | If you have come to a dead stop and you cannot think of where to go, explain where you are in the story and take five suggestions from the group. |

*Alliteration*: when two or more words in a sentence or poem begin with the same letter or sound. Used to create an impact on the reader

# UNIT 3 *Stop the Train*
## by Geraldine McCaughrean

In this unit you will learn about the following key objectives:

**Extract information** – learning how to use a range of reading strategies to extract information

**Character, setting and mood** – learning how to comment on the way writers convey setting, character and mood through their choice of words and sentences

**Independent reading** – developing your skills of critical reflection through personal response to the text

**Reflective writing** – writing reflectively about a text, taking account of the needs of others who might read it

**Explore in role** – developing drama techniques to explore in role a variety of situations

## Novel ideas

This unit focuses on the novel and the way the writer makes a story come alive. You will be looking at extracts from *Stop the Train* and learning how to improve your reading techniques. You will keep a reading journal, create a website and step into the shoes of the characters. You can also read this revealing interview with the author:

**Geraldine McCaughrean**

Where does Geraldine McCaughrean find her ideas and how does her imagination create the very different worlds of *The Kite Rider*, *Too Big* and *Stop the Train*?

> The whole book came to me in a revelationary flash. After that it just wrote itself. It was so infinitely more enjoyable to write than anything else I have written recently that it cost me no pain at all, and I was so unwilling to leave it behind at the end that I immediately went on to write a screenplay of it. ...The characters just walked into the book and said their lines: all I had to do was take dictation. ...*Stop the Train* is probably closest of all my books to fact, in that the town of Enid, Oklahoma, suffered a very similar dilemma in the early days of its existence.           Geraldine McCaughrean, September 2002

Taking on water, dropping off passengers and delivering supplies are all vital functions of the new steam links across America. Without the train, pioneers had a desperate fight to survive. *Stop the Train* follows the efforts of the first settlers of Florence, America to make the railroad stop at their town.

## Keeping a reading journal

A reading journal allows you to keep a record of your thoughts and feelings as you read a book. Keeping a reading journal will help you to learn not only about the book you are reading but about the actual reading process itself.

In a reading journal, you should:

- Ask questions
- Make predictions
- Include your thoughts and feelings
- Make connections with other books and other experiences
- Empathise with the characters
- Reflect on memorable moments
- Comment on the language

But you should not:

- Tell the story

# Cover story

How many times have you been tempted to read a book by its cover? What can it tell you? This is the cover of a paperback of *Shane* by Jack Schaefer.

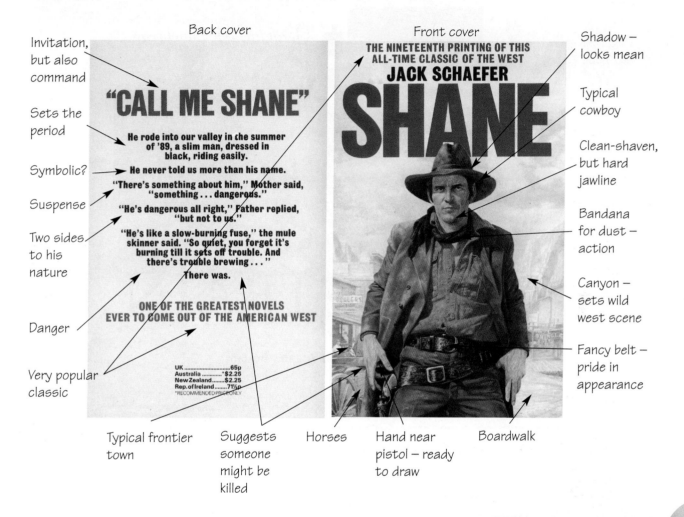

Back cover

Front cover

Invitation, but also command

Sets the period

Symbolic?

Suspense

Two sides to his nature

Danger

Very popular classic

THE NINETEENTH PRINTING OF THIS ALL-TIME CLASSIC OF THE WEST
JACK SCHAEFER
SHANE

"CALL ME SHANE"

He rode into our valley in che summer of '89, a slim man, dressed in black, riding easily.

He never told us more than his name.

"There's something about him," Mother said, "something . . . dangerous."

"He's dangerous all right," Father replied, "but not to us."

"He's like a slow-burning fuse," the mule skinner said. "So quiet, you forget it's burning till it sets off trouble. And there's trouble brewing . . ."

There was.

ONE OF THE GREATEST NOVELS EVER TO COME OUT OF THE AMERICAN WEST

UK ..................65p
Australia ............*$2.25
New Zealand......$2.25
Rep. of Ireland........71½p
*RECOMMENDED PRICE ONLY

Shadow – looks mean

Typical cowboy

Clean-shaven, but hard jawline

Bandana for dust – action

Canyon – sets wild west scene

Fancy belt – pride in appearance

Typical frontier town

Suggests someone might be killed

Horses

Hand near pistol – ready to draw

Boardwalk

# TASK

❶ Write down **five** questions about this book in your journal. E.g. Why is he so secretive?

❷ What makes you pick up a book and read on?

This is the original cover of *Stop the Train* by Geraldine McCaughrean.

What other books
has she written?

Why did it
win a prize?

How has the
artist used
colour?

How does
the text try
to 'hook' the
reader?

Why is
the train
shadowy?

What
does this
suggest?

What does
this suggest
about the
characters?

What does
the title
mean?

What do you
think the book
will be about?

Where can
I find more
reviews?

**Jacket illustration by Larry Rostant**

# TASK

Compare this dust jacket with the *Shane* cover. Which do you prefer
and why?

| *Shane* | *Stop the Train* |
| --- | --- |
| This is more/less effective because: | This would/would not attract me because: |

## Getting on track – Chapter 1

Once you have chosen your book, where do you start? Most of us look at the front cover, read the blurb and then skim the first page. We tend to pick up clues which hook us into reading on.

❶ Read the opening to *Shane* by Jack Schaefer.
❷ What sort of questions and thoughts run through your head as you read?
❸ Which words create pictures and which ones suggest the story to come?

### *Shane*

He rode into our valley in the summer of '89. I was a kid then, barely topping the backboard of father's old chuck-wagon. I was on the upper rail of our small corral, soaking in the late afternoon sun, when I saw him far down the road where it swung into the valley from the open plain beyond.

*Is this real?*

*Is this a western?*

*Why doesn't he have a name?*

In that clear Wyoming air I could see him plainly, though he was still several miles away. There seemed nothing remarkable about him, just another stray horseman riding up the road toward the cluster of frame buildings that was our town. Then I saw a pair of cowhands, loping past him, stop and stare after him with a curious intentness.

*Why did the writer start with him in the distance?*

*What's he doing there?*

*Why do they do this?*

He rode easily, relaxed in the saddle, leaning his weight lazily into the stirrups. Yet even in this easiness was a suggestion of tension. It was the easiness of a coiled spring, of a trap set.

*What is lurking underneath?*

*Is he dangerous?*

**❶** Now read the opening of *Stop the Train*.

**❷** How does the writer create the hooks which make us want to read on?

## *Stop the Train*

Like a bad-tempered queue-jumper, the train rolled up against its buffers and gave a vicious jolt. Then it gave in the opposite direction – a jerk which travelled from one coach to the next, tipping passengers back into their seats or forward out of them. Skillets and coffee pots clattered to the floor. Above Cissy's head, a pair of spurs scraped on the carriage roof, and a saddle slithered past the window, flailing its stirrups. But still the train did not move off. From end to end came the noise of men and children imitating the guard's whistle, but another ten minutes crawled by without the train making a move, and every second the carriage became hotter and hotter.

'I paid for first class tickets!' protested a latecomer, hopping up and down outside the carriage door in a red-faced rage.

'All first class on thissun,' said the guard and he offered the latecomer a leg-up on to the roof. 'Make room. 'nother one a-coming!' he announced cheerily, and there was a crump and an outburst of curses from over Cissy's head. She had never in her life heard so many curses as she had heard today.

Though she had been straining her ears for the sound all morning, Cissy never did hear the cannon, pistol-shot, or whatever signal it was that set things moving. That was drowned out by the noise of the whistlers and the groaning old people and the crying babies and the quarrelling children and the cries of, '...bought a first-class ticket...!' The train simply gave another shuddering jerk, blew its own whistle, and set off.

A roar swept down the train – a roar of excitement and relief mixed with protests as those on the roof were enveloped in steam and smuts from the funnel. The faces and fluttering handkerchiefs of well-wishers fell away, and beyond the window views opened up of flat unbroken prairies infested with moving figures.

# TASK

**❶** Record your thoughts and feelings in your reading journal. Comment on:
- ❏ The importance of the first pages of the book
- ❏ What we expect the writer to tell us
- ❏ What makes it a good beginning

**❷** Which of the following reading strategies did you use?

| Strategy | ✓ | ✗ | What you do ... |
|---|---|---|---|
| Scanning | | | |
| Skimming | | | |
| Drawing on experience | | | |
| Visualisation | | | |
| Re-reading | | | |

# Welcome to Florence – Chapters 2–4

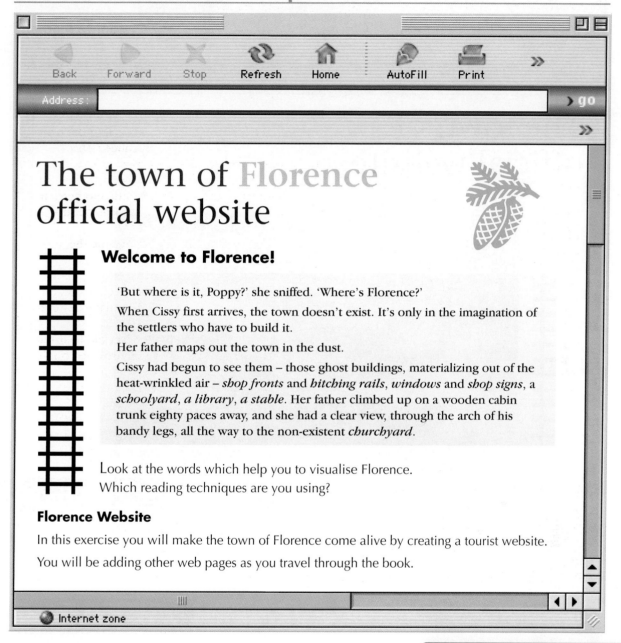

## The town of Florence official website

### Welcome to Florence!

'But where is it, Poppy?' she sniffed. 'Where's Florence?'

When Cissy first arrives, the town doesn't exist. It's only in the imagination of the settlers who have to build it.

Her father maps out the town in the dust.

Cissy had begun to see them – those ghost buildings, materializing out of the heat-wrinkled air – *shop fronts* and *hitching rails*, *windows* and *shop signs*, a *schoolyard*, *a library*, *a stable*. Her father climbed up on a wooden cabin trunk eighty paces away, and she had a clear view, through the arch of his bandy legs, all the way to the non-existent *churchyard*.

Look at the words which help you to visualise Florence.
Which reading techniques are you using?

### Florence Website

In this exercise you will make the town of Florence come alive by creating a tourist website.

You will be adding other web pages as you travel through the book.

## TASK

Chapters 2 and 3 of *Stop the Train* contain all the information you need to start plotting your own map of Florence. Use your scanning skills to locate the details.

**Now complete the web page on your handout.**

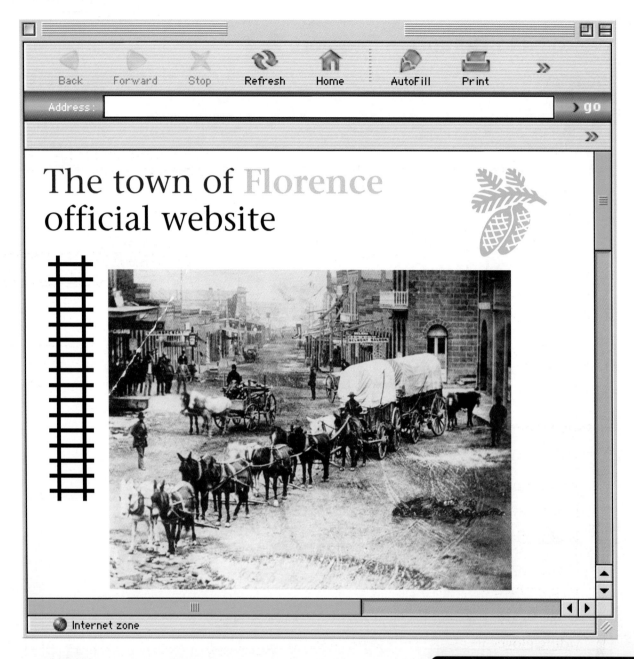

# The town of Florence official website

## TASK

Next, read Kookie's introduction to the characters.

Select appropriate information to fill out the blank 'Local Celebrities' web page.

You could also use Herman the Mormon's signs in Chapter 4 of *Stop the Train* to help you identify the occupations of the key characters.

You can add to the website at any time as you read the text.

## Shades of meaning – Chapter 5

How does the writer introduce a new character?

As time goes by, the townsfolk realise the need for a new schoolteacher and this advertisement appears in the *New York Tribune*:

> **God-fearing school teacher wanted for growing school,**
>
> **Florence, Cherokee Strip, Oklahoma State.**
>
> Salary by mutual arrangement.

Sven Magnusson, the baker, shocks the Florence ladies by also placing an advertisement for a replacement wife.

## TASK

Who will apply? Create a snapshot in your imagination!

Eventually the stagecoach deposits two female strangers. As you read the passage, imagine the reactions of the townsfolk. What were they expecting? Will these women be suitable?

> One of the ladies was a <u>slim needle</u> of a woman with <u>plump</u>, <u>pink cheeks</u>, wearing a <u>crushed bonnet</u> and <u>net gloves</u>. The other wore a <u>bright yellow plaid</u> underskirt, her iris-blue overdress caught up behind into <u>a bustle</u> so <u>extravagant</u> that it resembled a bunch of daffodils sprung from a ledge above the sea. A pair of <u>old scarlet leather riding gloves</u> were tucked into her waistband, and her hair was hardly less <u>red</u>.
>
> 'Oh my,' breathed Amos Warboys. 'Who's that?'

## TASK

❶ How do we judge characters?
❷ What sort of clues do we look for? You can annotate your copy by underlining the clues and noting what they suggest.

In pairs compare and contrast your impressions of the two ladies.

**Miss Harriet Pim**      **Mrs Loucien Shades**

❶ Read the full extract in your copy of the novel.

❷ Complete the chart below in your reading journal.

|  | What they notice | What they think |
|---|---|---|
| *The children* | The cheroot | Cissy is very concerned because this is not the sort of behaviour… |
| *The women* | The clothes | In those days a teacher would have dressed… |
| *The men* | The effects of the corset | Mrs Shades has a very 'statuesque' figure which is… |

You can find more information about Mrs Shades as a teacher in Chapters 7, 9 and 14 of *Stop the Train*.

**Reading strategy check: Which skills did you use?**

# The power of the word – Chapters 6–7

As part of the ongoing battle between the people of Florence and the Red Rock Railroad, the editor of the *Medford Daybreak* prints the following editorial in his newspaper:

# *The Daybreak's Editor writes:*

Having my attention brought to certain libellous remarks concerning our fine city of Medford, your editor made it his business to investigate an odious rag entitled *The Florence Morning Star*. I found it full of enough falsehoods to make a cat laugh.

Of the town of origin, my dear reader, you will not have heard, so let me depict for you Florence, OK. It is a place fit only for grazing pigs and burying felons. So putrid are its streets that the excellent Red Rock Railroad will not stop there on any account, for fear of disease or violence befalling its passengers.

Its citizens are such heathens that they find no need of a church. Such a notorious crew of ne'er-do-wells roam the streets that the children go armed for their own protection. The Florentines are so devoted to strong liquor that they believe coffee to be an invention for the creosoting of fences.

Cockroach capital of the South, Florence boasts a hotel so lively with bedbugs that every morning, the blankets walk out-of-doors of their own accord. As for the so-called newspaper, I would not use it to line my parrot's cage, for fear it offend the bird's good taste. It is a lying rag and I am perplexed to know why good paper and ink are wasted on it, for no citizen of Florence is clever enough to read. It must be bought only to swat the flies which hang in clouds over this pestilential den of iniquity. I have it on good authority that the editor is an anarchist by persuasion and a villain by nature, and I fully expect his newspaper to report soon that he has been hanged for the villain he is.

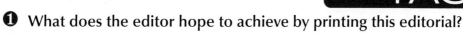

## TASK

❶ What does the editor hope to achieve by printing this editorial?

❷ How does he describe Florence and its townsfolk?

❸ How does this make you feel about the people of Florence?

❹ Now read the seven advertisements from the *Florence Morning Star* in the novel, which provoked this editorial. Apply active reading strategies to explore the way the writer uses words and sentences to create a positive image of Florence. Use the framework overleaf to structure your response.

| Writer | Extract |
|---|---|
| I think the writer is trying to… | by using… style |
| This … makes me feel… | because the writer… |
| The words… | create the impression that… |
| The other devices used, such as… | suggest… |

## Reading checklist

- [ ] Read between the lines
- [ ] Identify style or text type
- [ ] Decide whether this is the point of view of the author or a character
- [ ] Highlight
- [ ] Annotate
- [ ] Sift out key points
- [ ] Evaluate
- [ ] Visualise
- [ ] Read backwards and forwards

## Reading strategy check

- [ ] Which skills have you used today?

## Filmtrack – Chapters 8–12

The Wild West has always been a popular source of inspiration for the cinema. The early silent movies featured dastardly villains and helpless heroines. Last minute rescues had audiences sitting on the edge of their seats and weeping with relief.

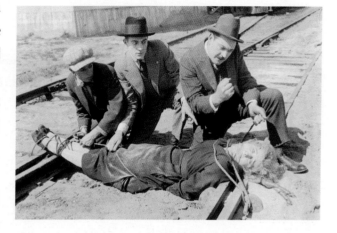

Many of these screenplays were adapted from the melodramas of travelling actors. Geraldine McCaughrean captures the thrill of such a performance in Chapter 7 of *Stop the Train*.

For the people of Florence, The Bright Lights Theatre Company's production of 'The Perils of Nancy' becomes larger than life.

If anyone could still recall paying ten cents to watch make-believe, in that instant they forgot. They were there, helpless witnesses to a cruel injustice. A silence fell as disturbing as the noise had been before.

The black-hearted landlord was able to lower his voice to a menacing hiss. *'But I know what will change your mind, my beauty! Aha*!' And binding young Nancy hand and foot with washline, he tied her to a railroad track painted on the hardboard stage.

Cissy buried her face in her father's lap. Frank Tate, remembering the RRR locomotive bearing down on him when he could not move, turned suddenly green and covered his mouth. Tibbie Boden ran out of the tent, sobbing, 'Stop him! Stop him somebody!' and finding herself alone on the empty prairie, ran back inside. Hildy Sissney dug her husband in the ribs and said, 'This is what will happen to us, you see if it don't!'

'Don't you hear the train, my beauty?' sneered the vile landlord. 'Submit or die!'

So Virgil Hobbs took out his Colt 45 and shot him.

In their determination to stop the train, two boys tie Tibbie Boden to the railway track. How does the author twist the emotions of the reader and build up suspense in this extract? In what ways is the description melodramatic? What do you see here? Whose eyes are you looking through?

> Sparks flew off the rail as Bob Eagle applied the brake. But his disgust at this latest ploy was so intense that he could only see the track ahead through red explosions of anger. He would slow his train, but he would not give them the satisfaction of sniggering and jeering at him, these little saboteurs. He would scare them so badly they would never want to see another locomotive so long as they lived. Where had they learned this little piece of melodrama? In the vaudeville halls? It was vile. It was childhood devilment turned to the Devil's work.

## TASK

❶ Visualise the images in the text here.
❷ What would you see if you were watching a film?
❸ What might you hear?

The viewpoint changes here. What happens to your view of the train?

> The great wheels slowed, but did not stop. Cissy turned round, smiling, breathless, to thank the driver, but saw the great engine still rolling, at walking speed. The whistle was ear-splitting; it made her duck, and cover her head. She tried to take a stand, between train and Tibbie, but the great iron bow of the cowcatcher pushed in among the hem of her dress and made her skip backwards. She saw, with a violent shudder, that a dead rabbit was wrapped around one fillet of the great iron grid. Did the man not realize how far the front of his train reached out ahead of the engine block? 'Stop! Stop! We can't get her free!' she yelled.

## TASK

❶ Visualise the images in the text here.
❷ What would you see if you were watching a film?
❸ What might you hear?

# All aboard the Red Rock Runner! – Chapters 13–14

In one of their most daring attempts, the Florence desperadoes succeed in hijacking the train and introducing the passengers to the delights of their town.

Here are some advertisements for entertainment planned for Florence Fair in Chapter 14 of *Stop the Train*.

**How far did the attractions fulfil their promise?**

---

**'HEAR THE CHOIR OF THE FLORENCE ACADEMY'**

———————

*'Enrich your sole with the works of W.J. Shakespear!'*

———————

*'JOIN WITH US ON A LANTERN-SLIDE TOUR OF THIS GREAT CONTENENT OF OURS'*

---

**TASK**

You are going to role play the reactions of the first tourists to Florence. Choose one of the characters below:

- The Mexican Catholic nun
- The school inspector
- A Texas rancher
- The big beef-fed gun salesman
- The homely woman with the turkey
- Neville T. Crupp (author of the Cherokee Strip)

Work in groups of four and imagine that you are four passengers travelling back in the carriage together. One of you is a reporter for the *Medford Gazette*. You will need to interview the others about the impromptu stop at Florence and find out what they saw or did as they visited the Fair.

As the visitors leave, they are treated to a free copy of the local paper, the *Florence Morning Star*. Inside, they read:

# An appeal on behalf of Florence, OK.

Have you enjoyed yourselves today? We earnestly hope it.

Come back next year, and it will be gone.

Have you seen things you like here? Met congenial folk? We rejoice at it. Come back next winter and they will be gone.

The town you have seen today has been shunned by the Red Rock Railroad.

Because of this, the citizens of Florence are on their beam ends. Their hopes and dreams can come to nothing so long as the town repines without a railroad.

We brought you here today to show you a town worth saving. For the sake of Florence, we intruded on your time, imposed upon your patience.

If, however, you were to speak kindly of us after today – if you were to tell your friends and kin that here is a town which deserves as much chance as her sister towns up and down the Medford-Amarillo line – then might Florence, OK yet be saved from the fate which overshadows her.

These things we respectfully ask you to grace with consideration on your homeward journey, for which we wish you GOD SPEED.

Nathaniel Rimm, EDITOR

## TASK

❶ Will you support the townsfolk?

❷ Be prepared to be hot seated by the rest of the group in the class railway carriage.

# Shoot out! – Chapters 15–16

One of the key themes in a Wild West drama is the showdown. For real life hero Wyatt Earp this was the gunfight at the OK Corral.

*Stop the Train* focuses on the long-running feud between Monterey and Boden.

The inhabitants of Florence are on tenterhooks waiting for the outcome of the fight!

> It was the day of the showdown – the gunfight between Jake Monterey and Gaff Boden, two enemies whose hatred had grown so all consuming nothing but blood could satisfy it.

## TASK

Plot out the position of the characters in the Florence incident in Chapter 15. You can add this to your website.

Why does the writer include bystanders and other characters in this part of the novel?

## TASK

Explore the way the writer builds up tension and creates a dramatic scene. The prompts in the table opposite will help you.

| A Setting the scene | B Characters |
|---|---|
| What details will be used to create local colour? | Is it important to describe what they are wearing? |
| Is the time of day important? | Will personality be shown through action? |
| Will the weather affect the mood? | What will their relationships show? |
| What is the atmosphere like? | Will dialogue be used? |
| How will this be suggested? | What will this suggest? |
| Is anyone else present? | Will there be a contrast? |
| | What will the reader be told? |
| | What effect do the main characters have on minor ones? |
| **C** The Grudge | **D** Building up tension |
| What is the cause of the fight? | What features of dialogue writing would help? |
| How long ago did it start? | What would suggest time passing? |
| Is there any way it can be resolved? | How will the tension in the characters be shown? |
| Is the grudge justified? | |
| What do the **protagonists** think of each other? | |
| What do others think of them? | |
| **E** Resolution | |
| Predict what will happen next in the story! | |
| How will the story close down ? | |

**Protagonist:** main character.

# TASK

Write your own closing paragraph. Be ready to share your ideas with the rest of the class!

## Sort out the Sheriff – Chapters 17–19

Wyatt Earp (pictured here) was probably the best known Sheriff in the Wild West. He was well respected by the townsfolk he served.

## TASK

**What qualities do you think would make a good sheriff?**

| Qualities | Reason |
|---|---|
| Literate | Needs to be able to read the wanted posters |

In Chapter 19 Florence suddenly finds itself without a sheriff.

**Name:** Klemme, Emile

**Age:** 34

**Experience:** Lawyer, used to settling legal disputes

**Qualities:** Firm, intelligent, devious, smug, reliable, shrewd, articulate, realist

**Appearance:** Smart, respectable, mature

# TASK

Imagine you are members of the committee studying the sheriff filing cards.

❶ In your groups make a short list of the three best candidates for the sheriff's job. Be prepared to justify your choices to the rest of the class.

❷ Would you choose this man? Marshall Haggar rides into Florence to sort out Jake, Gaff and Pickard after he hears about their shootout. What are your first impressions of him?

'I am Federal Marshall Haggar,' said the rider in the badge. He was a lardy, bulging man. His flesh bulged through the buttons of his shirt, over the belt of his trousers. Even his forearms bulged out of his riding gloves, his head out of his hat. His words, too, oozed out of him like melting lard. 'What happened to the water tower?' he asked, though patently he already knew. His look of disappointment said it all. His scene-of-crime had been wilfully tidied away; his evidence tampered with.

…Marshall Haggar referred to his pocket book again. 'Geoffrey Boden or Jake Monterey. Which of them ain't dead?' A startled murmur swept along the street. Boden? Monterey? 'Word is there was a gunfight hereabouts. The Law don't look kindly on gunfighting no more. It's clampin down,' said Marshall Haggar, and his fat top lip clamped down as if to demonstrate the rigor of the Law. 'These here ain't Frontier days no more. Frontier Law don't apply.' His small eyes darted around the assembled faces, accusing them, in a general way, of mischief.

## TASK

❶ How does Geraldine McCaughrean want us to feel about Marshall Haggar?

❷ Look at the words she uses and the effect they create.

❸ What effect does Marshall Haggar have on the mood in this chapter?

❹ Fill out your copy of the chart below.

| Evidence from text | Inference |
|---|---|
| Shot… a look of malicious contempt | He seems dangerous and vindictive. This creates a feeling of… |
|  |  |

❺ How does this chapter make you feel about the people of Florence?

❻ Review their behaviour in Chapter 18.

❼ Why does the writer create this impression?

# Author spotlight

Just how do writers start to create? How long does it take? Where does their inspiration come from?

▌▌ Only twice have I based a book on things that have really happened to ME. One was too big, after I bought a chest-of-drawers too big to fit up the stairs of our house and we had to employ a carpenter to take out a window before we could haul it inside. The other was Noah and Nelly in the Pet Pals series which relied on my sad experience of keeping fantail doves who all ended up in the stomach of the neighbourhood cats. ▌▌          Geraldine McCaughrean
• • • • • • • • • • • • • •

What questions would you like to ask your favourite author?

# TASK

❶ Jot down the questions in your reading journal.
❷ What questions would you ask Geraldine McCaughrean?
❸ You might start with the way she creates a story. Here she tells us how she approached her last book:

▌▌ *Kite Rider* entailed a lot of research, complex plotting, card-file indexing and so forth. It was quite a labour … *Stop the Train* was light relief, by comparison. It wrote itself. Besides, I was determined … to write a book that did not look as if it might be hard work to read. I wanted to keep the mood light and cheerful and funny. (I find, as a point of interest, that the more miserable you are in yourself, the easier it is to write a happy book, and vice versa.) ▌▌          Geraldine McCaughrean
• • • • • • • • • • • • • •

# TASK

❶ Once you have finished your questions, read the complete interview on the handout.

❷ Use a highlighter to identify useful information.

❸ Use a copy of the template below to record your findings.

| | |
|---|---|
| What I discovered about the writer | |
| What I learnt about the writing process | |
| Information about *Stop the Train* | |

## Time to reflect

How far were your questions answered? Do you have a clearer picture of the way a writer sets about the task? Were there any surprises?

# End of the Line – Chapter 20

Now that you have read to the end of the novel, look at your original predictions for the ending. Did you expect *Stop the Train* to end this way?

> *Deer Class 3,*
>
> *The werld dont seem hardly to have stood stil sinse the weeding. I hop you are all been good children for Miss May. You lissen up good, cos she ken teech you wot you need to no in life.*

## TASK

Share your impressions of this letter with a partner.

## TASK

❶ Answer these questions in your journal.

❑ Why do you think Geraldine McCaughrean leaves this letter to the final page?

❑ How does this alter your original impressions of the schoolteacher?

❑ Does it change your interpretation of events?

❑ If Miss May had arrived at the same time as Mrs Shades, would the story be different?

❑ How does Miss May compare with Mrs Shades?

**God-fearing school teacher wanted for growing school,**

**Florence, Cherokee Strip, Oklahoma State.**

Salary by mutual arrangement.

| Miss May | Mrs Shades |
|---|---|
| | |

Now you are going to explore the way the writer prepares the reader for the ending.

Loucien Shades
marries Everett Crew

↑

Emile Klemme
'jilts' Mrs Shades

↑

Everett Crew is
falsely accused of
being a traitor

↑

Everett Crew
arrives in
Florence with a
group of touring actors

↑

Loucien Shades
accepts the job
of schoolteacher

↑

Loucien Shades
arrives in Florence

## TASK

❶ **Choose one of these sub-plot endings and work backwards to when the characters enter the action. Use a flow diagram to identify the key steps of the story.**
  - ❑ **The Sissneys live happily ever after**
  - ❑ **Sheriff Klemme's double dealing is revealed**
  - ❑ **Jake Monterey becomes Sheriff**
  - ❑ **The railway stops at Florence**

  **As an example, the flow diagram for 'Loucien Shades marries Everett Crew' is shown here.**

❷ **Choose one storyline and alter the ending.**

## Freeze frame

Now you have finished reading *Stop the Train*, you are going to share your image of the text with the rest of the class. You will use a technique called *tableau vivant* which translates as 'living picture'.

Your aim is to present a scene from the book so that it looks like a still from a film.

You will need to **block** this to show the position of the characters and any props. It will look like a map from above.

**g** Blocking: to draw a sketch to show the position of the characters and props. Similar to a map from above.

# TASK

❶ Prepare your *tableau vivant*. You can use props to help suggest a character or scene. Once you have created your picture, you are not allowed to move until someone touches you. The rest of the class can then ask you questions about how you feel, what you are thinking, what has happened to you or what you are doing. You need to guess what you might be asked so that you can answer in character.

❷ List some possible questions the class might ask.

❸ Present your scene.

In this unit you will learn about the following key objectives:

**Clarify through talk** – shaping your ideas and helping you to think by speaking and listening to others

**Recall main points** – reflecting and commenting on the main points of a talk or reading

**Report main points** – reporting the main ideas so that you are able to agree on a course of actions following discussion

**Subordinate clauses** – extending your use and control of more complicated sentences

**Vary formality** – selecting appropriate formal or informal language depending on the circumstances

KEY OBJECTIVES

How good are you at expressing your views? Can you express your ideas to anyone? Can you back up your opinions? Are you able to challenge other people's views? This unit will help you to express your thoughts and opinions on some important issues. You will be exploring a group of poems about life in a city area. Whether you live in the city, a town or village or in the heart of the countryside you will build up your skills to talk clearly, to think about issues and to ask questions.

To improve your speaking skills you also need to listen carefully and understand what others have said. You need to remember their main ideas if you want to discuss them or to challenge them.

There are also times when you need to speak and write differently, depending on your audience. You probably chat to your friends in a very *informal* voice. However, you would expect a television news presenter to use a more *formal* style. This unit will allow you to practise using both *formal* and *informal* voices through a range of activities building up to a final radio presentation.

**First, meet Alice**

## In the high-rise Alice dreams of Wonderland

She received a parcel through the post.
It had everything she wanted inside it.
Sometimes when she touched it
A planet-sized man would come to the door
And say exactly the right kind of thing.
The parcel kept her happy,
Provided all she needed.
Her children blossomed,
Grew fat and pink and healthy.
The high-rise in which she lived shrank,
Became a neat house –
A swing on the lawn, a driveway etc. etc. etc.
A bill for the parcel arrived on Monday
On Tuesday came a reminder.
On Wednesday came a solicitor's letter.
On Thursday came a court order.
On Friday the jury gave a verdict.
On Saturday the parcel was taken.
Most days
Alice can be seen in the high-rise,
Mouth twisted, weeping.

## TASK

❶ With a partner, discuss what the 'parcel' means to Alice. What sort of things does she dream about? What happens to her dream of a perfect life?

❷ In pairs, role play Alice talking to a sympathetic neighbour about her situation and the dreams she has for herself and her children. Both will speak in a chatty, informal style, e.g. 'Morning, Alice. How's it going?', 'Not so good Clare. The baby's got an awful cold', 'I just wish the children had somewhere nice to play'.

Imagine that Alice has had trouble paying the rent. She receives this letter of eviction:

Stoney and Slate, Solicitors
1 Coombe House
Fleetchester
FC7 3SP

Ms Alice Parks                                              25 April 2003
307 High Towers
Fleetchester

Dear Madam,

Notice of Eviction

**I regret to inform you** that I have been **advised by** my client, Mr Screwham, **to serve notice on your tenancy** at 307 High Towers.

**Owing to substantial rent arrears** you are required to **vacate the premises** by midnight on Friday 23 May 2003. Failure to do so will result in personal property to the value of your rent arrears being **removed from the premises**.

Should you be in the position to **discharge the debt of** three months' rent arrears before 23 May 2003 your eviction date will be cancelled.

Yours faithfully,

*T A Stoney*

T A Stoney (Solicitor)

# TASK

In pairs, role play Alice discussing with her neighbour what she should do. Her Social Security cheque does not cover the rent. She is proud and hates depending on others. She will not resort to crime. She would consider work, but what about finding a child-minder? Again, you will speak in an informal, chatty style. For example, 'I've got to get a job, Clare. You know you said you'd mind the kids for me?'

As you could probably see, the solicitor's letter is written in very formal language that most of us are unlikely to use when speaking. It says 'I regret to inform you' which, when spoken, would be something like 'I'm sorry to say' or 'I'm sorry to tell you'.

Formal language of this kind contains no slang, no chatty expressions, no local dialect and (often) no feelings! It *should* be understood by anyone who speaks English, but it often uses difficult expressions, precise vocabulary and complex sentences which can make it difficult to follow.

It is important to understand very formal language because it is used on official forms and for business. Letters from a bank, a solicitor, your local council and your employer is likely to be written in this formal style.

## TASK

Look at the phrases that have been emboldened in the solicitor's letter. Copy the grid below, then change the formal language into an informal, chatty style. You may have to look up some of the formal words in a dictionary. One example has been done for you:

| Formal language | Informal language |
|---|---|
| I regret to inform you | |
| advised by | |
| to serve notice on your tenancy | |
| Owing to substantial rent arrears | |
| vacate the premises | |
| removed from the premises | taken from the flat |
| discharge the debt of | |

## TASK

In pairs, prepare a role play of Alice talking to the solicitor and asking for an extension on the period of notice. Alice will speak in an informal style but the solicitor will use some of the formal phrases listed above.

Alice sees this job advertised in the local paper and decides to apply for it. She writes a very sensible letter, but she writes as she speaks. Alice needs some help to write a more formal letter.

**Manager for
Fashion Boutique
required**

Must have a good education, relevant retail experience, be of presentable appearance and have good communication skills.
Send letter and CV to....

*307, High Towers,
Fleetchester*

*Dear Madam,*

*<u>There's a job for</u> Manager of the Fashion Boutique in the local press that I would like to <u>have a go at</u>.*

*I am 22 years old and have <u>a lot of</u> experience <u>working in shops</u>. When I left school I <u>done</u> 3 years work in Fitright Shoes as a shop assistant. I <u>would of</u> become manageress but I decided to have kids instead. Now my two <u>kids</u> are <u>down</u> the Nursery from 9–3. <u>Like I said</u>, I can <u>have a go</u> at being a Manager...*

# TASK

❶ Help Alice to rewrite her letter of application by altering the informal expressions which are underlined and using more formal language. For example, the opening sentence might read: With regard to the position of Manager of the Fashion Boutique advertised in the local newspaper, I would like to apply for the post…

❷ Then complete her letter including information about her education, personal qualities and suitability for the post. *Let's hope Alice is lucky!*

# Out in the city

This next poem celebrates city life. The boy in this poem loves his city world.

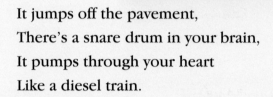

### *Out in the City*

When you're out in the city
Shuffling down the street,
A bouncy city rhythm
Starts to boogie in your feet.

It jumps off the pavement,
There's a snare drum in your brain,
It pumps through your heart
Like a diesel train.

There's Harry on the corner,
Sings, 'How she goin' boy?'
To loose and easy Winston
With his brother Leroy.

Shout, 'Hello,' to Billy Brisket
With his tripe and cows' heels,
Blood stained rabbits
And trays of live eels.

Maltese Tony
Smoking in the shade
Keeping one good eye
On the amusement arcade.
And everybody's talking:

Move along
step this way
Here's a bargain
What you say
Mind your backs
Here's your stop
More fares
Room on top.

*continued*

Neon lights and take aways
Gangs of boys and girls
Football crowds and market stalls
Taxi cabs and noise

From the city cafes
On the smokey breeze
Smells of Indian cooking
Greek and Cantonese

Well some people like suburban life
Some people like the sea
Others like the countryside
But it's the city
Yes it's the city
It's the city life
For me.

Gareth Owen

# TASK

❶ What sort of rhythm does the poem have? Why is it written like this?

❷ How can you tell the difference between the narrator's 'voice' and the voices of the city people?

❸ In the grid below, there are two columns. Copy the grid and then list the things that the narrator enjoys about city life in the first column. In the second column, think of ways you could challenge the narrator's views. The first two have been done for you.

| |
|---|---|
| • Lively atmosphere<br>• Interesting characters (Billy Brisket, Maltese Tony, etc.)<br>•<br>•<br>•<br>• | • Too much noise!<br>• Interesting characters can be seen anywhere, not only in the city<br>•<br>•<br>•<br>• |

# Subordinate clauses

So much depends on the way you speak. While you probably find it easy to chat in an informal way to friends, it is not so easy to speak in a formal style or to express yourself using more complex sentences.

We tend to speak using a chain of 'ands'. For example, *I went to the pictures and I saw Will Smith in* Men in Black 2 *and it was really good*. However, writing and speech can be made more interesting by the use of **subordinate clauses**. A simple sentence like 'Samina enjoyed visiting London' can be improved by adding detail with a subordinate clause and so becomes a complex sentence:

> *Samina enjoyed visiting London although she found it expensive.*

Here a connective 'although' introduces the subordinate clause. It is subordinate or dependent on the main clause or sentence because 'although she found it expensive' is not a complete sentence in itself.

## TASK

❶ With a partner, practise adding a subordinate clause to *Samina enjoyed visiting London.* Add it *after* the main clause using some of the connectives in the box.

| whenever | if | because | unless |
|----------|-----|---------|--------|
| but | when | since | while |
| with | as | after | although |
| where | in case | as long as | until |

❷ Now practise starting your sentence with the conjunction and finishing with the main clause, for example:

> <u>**Since she had passed her driving test,**</u> *Samina enjoyed visiting London.*

Notice the comma has to be added after the subordinate clause.

❸ Subordinate clauses can also begin with the relative pronouns 'who' or 'which'. In this example, extra detail about the subject is sandwiched inside the main clause:

> *Samina, <u>who had just passed her driving test,</u> enjoyed visiting London.*

Notice that two commas have been used to 'embed' the subordinate clause in the sentence.

With a partner, practise adding a subordinate clause starting with 'who' or 'which' to the following sentences (after the noun):

- The dog barked loudly.
- Andy played the piano with skill.
- The girl yawned rudely.
- Cars will be towed away.

When you add subordinate clauses you are making sentences more complex.

# Where you live

Like Gareth Owen's character in the poem 'Out in the City', the writer and traveller, Bill Bryson, loves city life. In his book *Notes from a Small Island* Bill Bryson explains why he loves the city of London.

I can never understand why Londoners fail to see that they live in the most wonderful city in the world. It is far more beautiful and interesting than Paris, if you ask me, and more lively than anywhere but New York – and even New York can't touch it in lots of important ways. It has more history, finer parks, a livelier and more varied press, better theatres, more numerous orchestras and museums, leafier squares, safer streets and more courteous inhabitants than any other large city in the world.

And it has more congenial small things – incidental civilities you might call them – than any other city I know: cheery red pillar boxes, drivers who actually stop for you on pedestrian crossings, lovely forgotten churches with wonderful names like St Andrew by the Wardrobe and St Giles Cripplegate, sudden pockets of quiet like Lincoln's Inn and Red Lion Square, interesting statues of obscure Victorians in togas, pubs, black cabs, double-decker buses, helpful policemen, polite notices, people who will stop to help you when you fall down or drop your shopping, benches everywhere. What other great city would trouble to put blue plaques on houses to let you know what famous person once lived there or warn you to look left or right before stepping off the kerb? I'll tell you. None.

## TASK

❶ On your copy of the text, highlight all the things that Bill Bryson enjoys about London.

❷ In pairs, work out two or three sentences that each of you can say to sum up Bill Bryson's love of this capital city. Use a subordinate clause in each one, e.g. 'Although it is not as lively as New York, London is livelier than anywhere else.'

❸ Now report back to the rest of the class. Explain how you have used complex sentences.

Prepare a two-minute speech which celebrates the area in which you live. If you prefer you can focus on the bad aspects of where you live but this may be more difficult. Use the following plan to help you to prepare your ideas:

---

### Planning a speech

- Start with an introduction. Explain where you live; its geographical location; how long you have lived there; who you live with etc.
- List three or four things you intend to focus upon, e.g. friends, family, favourite places, shops, interesting characters, facilities, school, clubs, games you play and where you play them. Each one will be dealt with now in a separate bullet
- The best thing about living in your area …
- The next best thing …
- The third best thing …
- Your overall conclusion

---

Your speech should be in formal language, using Standard English and avoiding slang or chatty expressions. Here are some suggestions for appropriate language you might use:

---

### Useful phrases

- Living in … has many advantages …
- The person whom I appreciate the most is …
- There are several activities (places, games) which I enjoy such as …
- The principal reason for this is …
- One of the places which I frequently visit is … because …
- Consequently, living in … has many advantages.
- To conclude…

### Alternative words to use

- Instead of 'I like' try using *I'm fond of, I relish, I revel in, I appreciate*
- Instead of 'my favourite' *try my most valued, my preferred* (activity, game, etc.)
- Instead of 'best' try *chief, foremost, leading, principal*
- Instead of 'used to' try *in the habit of, accustomed to, familiar with, at home in*
- For 'a lot' try *several, many*

---

Where you live is very important to you. It should bring you security and pleasure. However, there are many people for whom city life means poverty and homelessness. The following information is adapted from the website of Crisis, a charity that helps homeless people.

Crisis is the national charity for homeless people, especially those who don't 'qualify' for statutory support. Our goal is to alleviate the poverty and distress experienced by the homeless as they have literally nowhere else to turn, neither friends, family nor state. We provide lasting solutions to homelessness.

We work year-round to help vulnerable people through the crisis of homelessness, rebuild their lives, reintegrate into society and live independently.

Crisis was founded in 1967, in response to the shocking television documentary *Cathy Come Home*.

Homelessness is a complex issue and affects those sleeping on the streets or staying in temporary accommodation, hostels, bed & breakfasts etc. Sadly some people are more at risk than others of becoming homeless because of their background, circumstances and events facing them. This includes people leaving care and those with mental health problems.

There are 400,000 hidden homeless people in England, staying in hostels, B&Bs and squats. They live in often appalling conditions, without security, privacy or any real hope of a better future or somewhere to call home. Their problems are numerous and include alcohol, mental health and increasingly drug addiction as well as loneliness, lack of self-confidence or skills. Their conditions of life are often appalling.

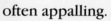

# TASK

When you have read this text, discuss it with a partner. Identify the problems faced by homeless people. Which do you think are the most serious and why?

# Unlucky for some

The following poems are from a group of 13 poems by Roger McGough called 'Unlucky for Some'. The poems all have 13 lines and each one deals with a character who is homeless or down on their luck.

**1**

What do I do for a living? Survive.
Simple as that. 'God helps those
who help themselves.' That's what the Vicar
told me. So I went into
the supermarket and helped myself.
Got 6 months. God helps those
who help themselves. Nowadays
I'm a traveller. Southwest mainly
then back here for the winter.
I like the open air. Plenty of it
and it's free. Everything else I beg
borrow or steal. Keep just about alive.
What do I do for a living? Survive.

**2**

It's the addicts I can't stand.
Getting drunk on pills. Stoned
they call it. Make me sick.
Sticking needles into themselves
in dirty lavatories. Got no shame.
And they get prescriptions. Wish
my doctor would give me one
every time I felt like a drink.
I could take it along to the
allnight off licence in Piccadilly
come back here and get drunk
for a week. Get high. Stoned.
It's the addicts I can't stand.

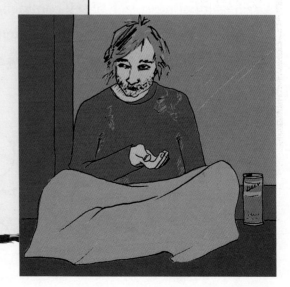

**3**

First and foremost I need a coat.
The one I'm wearing's got patches
on the patches. I can't go
for interviews dressed like this.
What sort of a job do you think
I'd get? A job as a tramp?
No thank you. And while I'm here
I need some vests and knickers.
None of them fancy ones either.
And shoes. Two pair. Leather.
Don't argue, I know my rights.
Refuse and I'll take you to court.
First and foremost I need a coat.

**4**

Oh no. I don't have to be here.
I'm not a cast-off like the rest.
I'm one of the lucky ones. I've got
children. Both grown up. A son
and daughter who'd be only too pleased
to have me living with them
But I prefer my independence.
And besides, they've got their own lives.
I'd only have to pick up the phone
and they'd be over. Or send money.
I mean, I could afford a room
in a nice clean hotel somewhere.
Oh no. I don't have to be here.

**❶** Read the four poems carefully. In pairs, discuss the following questions:

A   What reasons can you find in the poems for each character being homeless or down on their luck?

B   Which characters do you think are the toughest and most vulnerable? Find evidence to support your opinions.

C   Some people who are homeless or with no source of income choose to sell *The Big Issue* to make a living. Read the information about it on the next page. Do you think any of the characters in the poems would choose to sell it? Why? Would it change their lives if they did?

**❷** Copy the following grid and use it to note your answers to the questions above. The characters in the four poems have simply been numbered but you could give them names. Some of the grid has already been completed for you.

|  | 1 Jimmy | 2 | 3 | 4 |
|---|---|---|---|---|
| **Question A** | After release from prison, became traveller. Likes open air: 'Plenty of it and it's free' |  |  |  |
| **Question B** |  |  | Very assertive – 'I know my rights' |  |
| **Question C** |  |  |  |  |

## *What have we achieved?*

The Big Issue Magazine sells 250,000 copies a week and is read by over 1 million people. The Big Issue has given literally thousands of homeless people the opportunity to earn a legitimate income and stand on their own two feet. It has put millions of pounds straight into their hands and given homeless people a route out of poverty and exclusion. It proves that business can do social good. It has also radically shifted the general perception of homeless people. It has proved that given the opportunity, the disadvantged do want to improve themselves and make changes in their lives.

The foundation has given our vendors the opportunity to use the Big Issue as a stepping stone. A range of service provision, both within the Big Issue office and in partnership with specialist providers, means we can offer a comprehensive package to enable people to improve their lives.

**1** Look closely at the first poem on page 84, 'What do I do for a living? Survive.' Notice the following features:

❏ It is written in 13 lines (unlucky 13!)

❏ The last two lines rhyme. In the other poems the last two lines also rhyme or are 'half rhymes' like 'stoned/stand'. These do not quite rhyme because the main vowel sound is different, but they still sound very similar

❏ The poem tells you about the life and background of this homeless character – he has been in prison; he is probably an old style tramp who walks from the countryside to the city in the winter; he lives by his wits and is prepared to beg, borrow or steal

❏ It is written in the first person using the voice of the character in the poem. His normal, chatty language style is used

**2** Now write a similar 13-line poem about a character who is down on his or her luck. The box below has some suggestions about the types of characters you could choose:

---

**Some suggestions for characters**

- A taxi driver who has lost his licence
- An out-of-work actor who remembers his or her past glories
- A bankrupt person who has had a nervous breakdown because he or she cannot face financial ruin
- A teenager who has run away to the big city but who cannot find work

---

**3** In groups of four, read your poems aloud. Listen to each poem carefully. Note the main features of each character's life and background. Select one poem from your group of four to be read out to the class. Using your notes, describe the features of the chosen character and explain why you have selected this poem.

You are building up the skills for your final major task, which will require you to write and speak about several aspects of city life. The following task provides a further opportunity to explore homelessness. It is based on characters you met in 'Unlucky for Some'.

Remember, you can make your language more interesting by placing subordinate clauses in different positions in a sentence, for example:

**a** Jimmy returned to the city in the winter, <u>carrying all his possessions on his back</u>.
<u>Carrying all his possessions on his back</u>, Jimmy returned to the city.

**b** Doris, <u>banging her fist on the table</u>, demanded a pair of shoes.
<u>Banging her fist on the table</u>, Doris demanded a pair of shoes.

What is the effect of putting the subordinate clauses in these different places? What do you notice about the punctuation?

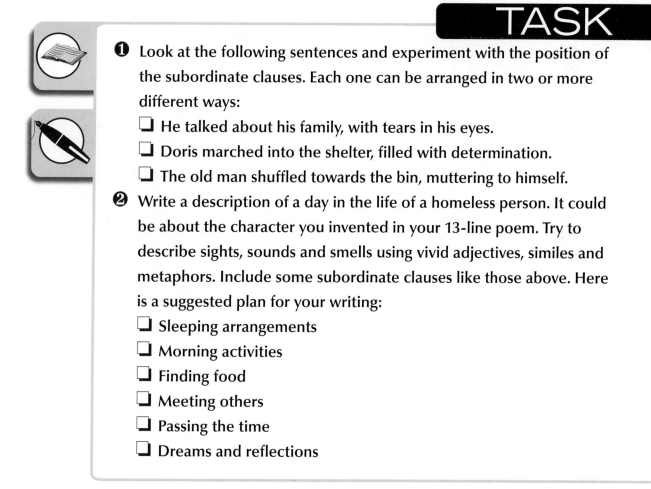

# TASK

❶ Look at the following sentences and experiment with the position of the subordinate clauses. Each one can be arranged in two or more different ways:
  ❑ He talked about his family, with tears in his eyes.
  ❑ Doris marched into the shelter, filled with determination.
  ❑ The old man shuffled towards the bin, muttering to himself.

❷ Write a description of a day in the life of a homeless person. It could be about the character you invented in your 13-line poem. Try to describe sights, sounds and smells using vivid adjectives, similes and metaphors. Include some subordinate clauses like those above. Here is a suggested plan for your writing:
  ❑ Sleeping arrangements
  ❑ Morning activities
  ❑ Finding food
  ❑ Meeting others
  ❑ Passing the time
  ❑ Dreams and reflections

# Radio documentary about city life

The next task will bring together all the skills you have been working on so far. You will create a radio documentary about city life for your local radio station. It should be aimed at a family audience, which is likely to include parents and children. You will have to:

- Speak clearly, expressing your ideas and asking appropriate questions
- Conduct interviews in which you show that you can listen to others and recall the main points of their talk so that you can challenge or build on their ideas
- Use both formal and informal language appropriately, depending on the circumstances
- Use complex sentences
- Collaborate in small groups of four people, agreeing your responsibilities and sharing the work so that it is completed in a given time

In groups of four you will have to decide who will take the following roles:

## 1  Presenter of the radio documentary

Your job will be to introduce the programme. You will agree a title for it and welcome listeners. You will explain what your documentary is about and provide an interesting summary so that listeners know what to expect and keep listening. Your language will be formal and you will use complex sentences and precise vocabulary, but you must make your voice sound lively by varying your tone. You will provide the links between various items in your documentary.

### Expressions you might use

Welcome to 'Inside Story', the programme that gives you in-depth information about...
City life can be stimulating or bleak, depending on the circumstances...
Our reporters have discovered individuals from several city locations...
We will be interviewing Jimmy, who has been homeless for 17 years...
Firstly...
Our next item consists of...
Finally we have...

## 2   The radio interviewer

Your job will be to interview at least two people. You will need to introduce your item/s by explaining who you are about to interview, their circumstances and why you chose to interview them. Draw up a list of questions that will help your interviewee to provide the information you need. This means listening carefully to their answers and building on them. If, for example, your question 'What is it like living in a hostel?' gets the response 'Not very nice', you will need to invite more information by adding something like: 'Describe what it is like for the listeners'. Your language will be formal, using complex sentences when you do your introduction, but your questions will be simple and clear.

### Expressions you might use

Have you ever wondered what it might be like living in a hostel (or on the streets)?
Some people find life in the city extremely exciting/stimulating/ entertaining…
Alice, can you explain to the listeners what living in the city is like…
Gareth, you appear to have very positive views about the city…
Where do you go for entertainment (or food shopping, or to church)?

## 3   Characters (at least two) to be interviewed

You will role play one of the characters you met earlier in the unit. It could be Alice, her neighbour, the solicitor (Mr Stoney), Gareth Owen (a lover of city life), one of the home-less characters or someone else who lives in the city. Your responses to questions will be informal (unless you are the solicitor) and you will have to work closely with the radio interviewer so that you are prepared.

### 4  Presenter of an item on the homeless

Your role is to prepare an item about the homeless as part of the same radio documentary. You will have to organise your item but instead of describing an individual, you will be talking generally about the homeless. You can refer to the articles from *Crisis* and the *Big Issue*. You may wish to interview a homeless person or someone who cares for the homeless. Your language will be formal, using complex sentences.

## Expressions you might use

Homelessness is a complex issue…

There are as many reasons for homelessness as there are people living on the streets…

The homeless, without a fixed address, are usually unable to find employment…

Too often people dismiss the topic of homelessness with blind prejudice…

There are charities which devote their services to alleviating the poverty and distress experienced by…

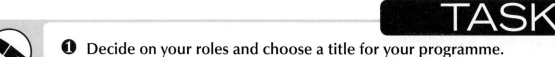

❶ Decide on your roles and choose a title for your programme.

❷ Plan your programme by deciding on a sequence of items and approximate timings.

❸ Write your own item or items.

❹ Help the interviewer to draw up a list of questions and prepare answers.

❺ Share the work and support each other.

❻ Rehearse the programme.

❼ Present your radio documentary to the rest of the class.

❽ Listen carefully to other presentations and note the parts played by each person, the different ways that formal and informal language are used, the main views presented, and any opinions and questions you might have. Share your comments, opinions and questions with the rest of the class.

# UNIT 5 The spelling detectives

**KEY OBJECTIVES**

In this unit you will learn about the following key objectives:

**Vowel choices** – making sure that you know the spelling patterns for the different vowel sounds in words

**Personal spelling** – learning how to apply spelling strategies to improve your own spelling

If you are going to become a really good speller, it is important to learn how to spell. This is much more useful than simply learning lists of words. When you know which strategies help you as a speller, you will have the confidence and the techniques to tackle even the words you find most difficult. To do this, you will be acting as a spelling detective: someone who investigates and finds solutions to even the most complicated spelling patterns.

To help you in your investigations, you will be shown ways to learn and remember a variety of spelling patterns. You will be capable of solving both your own and other pupils' spelling mysteries!

In order to record your investigations you will keep a spy notebook in which you will jot down your observations. You will be able to use and refer to this when you apply your spelling knowledge to other writing activities.

# Why does spelling matter?

Have you ever been in a situation where you had to spell a word that you simply did not know?

Fortunately, there are strategies that can help you in a situation like this. You might:

- Break the word into syllables. Remember that every syllable should have a vowel,
    e.g. re/mem/ber
- Break the word down using prefixes and suffixes. Long and seemingly difficult words can be broken down and built back up in this way,
    e.g. dis/satisfact/ion
- Use a mnemonic. Be careful though! It can be difficult to remember too many mnemonics. Save them for words that you cannot spell in any other way,
    e.g. necessary – a shirt has one **c**ollar and two **s**leeves
- Use spellspeak. Say the word as it appears rather than the way it is normally pronounced,
    e.g. Wed/nes/day
- Look for words within words,
    e.g. bu<u>sin</u>ess or defi<u>nite</u>
- Think about other words in the same family,
    e.g. govern/governess/government
- Work out the meaning of root words,
    e.g. triangle/tricycle/triplets/triceps (tri = three)

## TASK

❶ With a partner, decide which strategy might help you to spell the following words:
- ❏ conscience
- ❏ where
- ❏ vegetable
- ❏ television
- ❏ disappearance

❷ Record your three most helpful strategies in your spy notebook.

Another useful strategy is the 'Look, Cover, Say, Write, Check' method:

1   Look at the word – try to get a picture of it in your mind

2   Cover it up

3   Sound it out

4   Draw it in the air

5   Write it down

6   Check to see if it is correct

7   If it is correct, write it four more times

8   If it is wrong, underline the part of the word you had trouble with and try again until it is correct

9   Use it in a piece of writing as soon as possible

Look back at the spelling strategies on page 94. One strategy was spellspeak – sounding the word out as it appears on the page. In order to do this, you need to draw on your knowledge of phonics.

A phoneme is the smallest unit of sound in a word and we can use our phonic knowledge to break a word down into its separate sounds or phonemes. The word cat is made up of three separate phonemes: c – a – t. Sound out each separate phoneme and listen carefully to see how you can build the word out of its separate sounds.

## TASK

How many phonemes can you hear in these words? Remember, you are listening for separate sounds, not letters.
- Map
- Pick
- Catch
- Switch
- Damage

Phonics can help us with our spelling. If we can break a word down into its separate sounds, then we can also build the word up again, relating separate sounds to letters or strings of letters. Phonics will not help us to solve all our spelling problems, but they can certainly help.

## TASK

With a partner, look at the following words. Which words would your phonic knowledge help you to spell?
- Computer
- Clumsiness
- Supermarket
- Monologue
- Crashed
- Envelope
- Exclamation
- Atmosphere
- Script
- Thought

One of the difficulties in our spelling system is that although we have 26 letters in our alphabet, we have far more than 26 sounds. Of those 26 letters, only five of them are vowels. This means that those vowels have to work especially hard to join the sounds of the consonants together. The sound of the vowel in a word depends on the other letters around it. For example, listen to the difference between the sounds made by the letter **e** in the words **drew**, **pen** and **feel**.

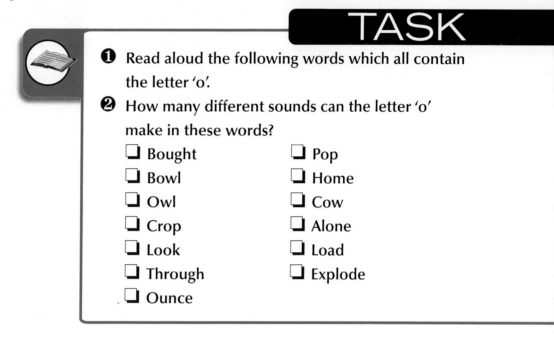

# TASK

❶ Read aloud the following words which all contain the letter 'o'.

❷ How many different sounds can the letter 'o' make in these words?

❏ Bought        ❏ Pop
❏ Bowl          ❏ Home
❏ Owl           ❏ Cow
❏ Crop          ❏ Alone
❏ Look          ❏ Load
❏ Through       ❏ Explode
❏ Ounce

If you look at the words in the task again you will notice that sometimes the letter 'o' appears next to another vowel.

When two vowels appear next to each other in a word (l**oa**d), this is known as a vowel digraph.

A split vowel digraph is when two vowels are split by a consonant, for example, h**o**m**e**.

# TASK

❶ Look at the list of words in the task above again. Pick out all the words which contain a vowel digraph.

❷ What effect do the vowel digraphs have on the way the letter 'o' is pronounced?

Those tricky vowel sounds are responsible for many of our spelling difficulties. Each vowel has a short sound and a long sound.

Their short sounds can be found in words like:

a = tap, wrap, pack, cat

e = bed, leg, egg, fed

i = pick, sing, lid, thin

o = dot, rock, modern, fog

u = muck, lug, rub, up

Their long sounds can be found in words like:

a = rail, gape, hate, day

e = leaf, heat, asleep, receive

i = mind, night, time, lie

o = grow, so, know, road

u = rude, you, drew, use

## The spelling detective investigates...

❶ Sound out the short and long sounds for each vowel. What differences can you hear? Can you hear the long vowel sounds saying their alphabet names?

❷ Work in groups to investigate the patterns of spelling in long vowel sounds.

❸ Choose one of the long vowel sounds – a, e, i, o, or u.

❹ Find as many words as you can which contain the long vowel sound and write them down. Use a dictionary.

❺ Note down the different ways of spelling the long vowel sound. For example, the long 'a' vowel sound is usually spelt: a-e, ai or ay.

❻ Work out:
- ❏ The most common spelling of the long vowel sound
- ❏ The most common spelling at the end of the word
- ❏ The most common spelling in the middle of the word
- ❏ The most common spelling when the vowel is split by a consonant

# The double rule

Now that you understand about short and long vowel sounds, you will be able to use this simple rule:

- Begining or beginning?
- Writter or writer
- Diner or dinner?

Here is the general rule:

- If it is a long vowel sound, use one consonant.
- If it is a short vowel sound, double the consonant.

It is important to remember this when you add vowel suffixes like -ing, -er, -ed and -est to the ends of words. You will need to double the last consonant if it comes after a vowel, for example, drag = dragged, wet = wettest. If the last consonant does not come after a vowel, do not double it, for example, scratch = scratching, help = helper.

Vowels can affect the way we pronounce consonants in words.

## TASK

❶ Work with a partner to find as many words as possible which contain the letter 'c' followed by a vowel. You should include the letter 'y' as a vowel for this task.

❷ Now sort your words into separate piles. Use the following headings:

ca   ce   c   co   cu   cy

❸ What do you notice about the way you pronounce the letter 'c' in the words in each pile?

❹ What is the effect of the vowel on the letter 'c'?

❺ Write your observations in your spy notebook.

# Hidden vowels

Some words contain vowels which are not always clearly pronounced. Here are a few. Can you think of any more?

- Family
- Wednesday
- Definite
- Interest
- Mathematics

- History
- Parliament
- Secretary
- Business

## TASK

❶ Work with a partner to identify the unstressed vowel in each word. It will help if you listen carefully as your partner sounds out the word. Take it in turns to do this.

❷ Look back at the spelling strategies on page 94. Which ones would help you to spell words with unstressed vowels?

❸ Make a note of these in your spy notebook.

### SPELLING NOTEBOOK

Last Wensday we went out to diner at a restaurant. It was my birthday and I was aloud to invite a frend. I decided to take Kalia becos I have nown her since primary school.

I was very exited about my birthday. I got a new pair of trainers and a CD player. They where my best presents. I had a lovley time and can't wate until next year.

Last Wensday we went out to diner at a restaurant. It was my birthday and I was aloud to invite a frend. I decided to take Kalia becos I have nown her since primary school.

I was very exited about my birthday. I got a new pair of trainers and a CD player. They where my best presents. I had a lovley time and can't wate until next year.

When we make spelling mistakes, it helps to identify the part of the word that we got wrong. Katy has made a number of mistakes in this short piece of writing.

## TASK

Read Katy's work and, on your copy, underline or highlight the part of each word she has spelt incorrectly.

You should have found ten mistakes.

## TASK

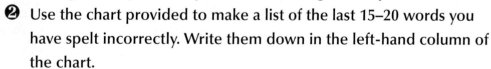

❶ With a partner, explore the part of the word Katy has trouble with.

❷ Which strategies would you suggest Katy should use to learn these words?

## TASK

❶ Look back over your last few pieces of written work. You should look through work you have produced in a range of subjects.

❷ Use the chart provided to make a list of the last 15–20 words you have spelt incorrectly. Write them down in the left-hand column of the chart.

❸ Check the correct spelling of each word and write it down in the right-hand column of the chart.

❹ Look carefully at your spelling errors. Can you see any patterns? For example, do you confuse words like there, they're and their? Or do you forget to change a 'y' to 'ies' in some plural words?

❺ Finally, identify three spelling strategies you could use to improve your personal spelling. Look back at the spelling strategies on page 94 to remind you. Record them in your spy notebook.

# Word building with affixes

We have already noted that prefixes and suffixes can help us to spell some tricky words.

Prefixes are groups of letters which are added to the beginnings of words. Suffixes are added to the ends of words. Prefixes and suffixes can change the meanings of words.

Here are some prefixes:

- contra-
- de-
- dis-
- inter-

- post-
- pre-
- re-
- sub-

## The spelling detective investigates...

**TASK**

❶ Work with a partner to find ten words which begin with these prefixes.

❷ What can you detect about:
- ❏ The meaning of the prefix?
- ❏ The impact of the prefix on the way the word is spelt?

> **Helpful hint**
>
> mis+spelt
> dis+satisfied
>
> The prefix is added to the root word. One 's' belongs to the prefix and one to the root word. How might this rule help you to spell 'unnecessary'?

Some prefixes change a word to its opposite meaning. They are:

- anti-
- un-
- im-

- il-
- ir-
- in-

Can you match the correct prefix to the following words to change them to their opposite meanings?

| | | |
|---|---|---|
| mature | clockwise | sociable |
| responsible | fair | biotic |
| legible | possible | adequate |
| credible | literate | regular |

## TASK

With a partner, work out the meanings of the following suffixes:

- -fy (purify, simplify)
- -ful (plentiful, beautiful)
- -less (careless, hopeless)
- -hood (childhood, knighthood)
- -ous (famous, courageous)
- -ly (happily, jokingly)

## The spelling detective investigates...

What happens to words ending in 'y' when the suffix is added?

What do you notice about the spelling of the suffix -ful?

## TASK

Use prefixes and suffixes to build words around the following roots:

- vent
- rupt
- port

# Homophones

Some words cause problems because they are easily confused with each other. They sound the same but have different spellings and meanings, for example: flour and flower; there and their; or rain and reign. These words are called homophones.

## TASK

❶ Write down as many pairs of homophones as you can think of.

❷ Choose one pair of homophones and produce a calligram which shows the difference between the two words. A calligram is a visual representation of a word that illustrates its meaning.

❸ Transfer a smaller version of your calligram to your spy notebook.

# Spelling investigation

**TASK**

❶ Work in groups to find words which contain the following letter strings. The letter strings may come from the begining, middle or endings or words.

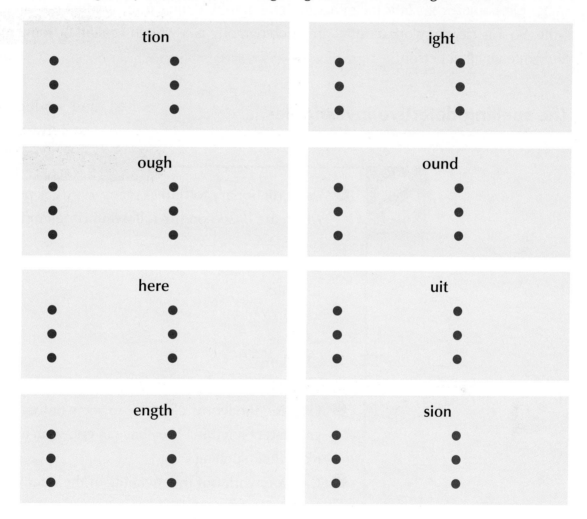

❷ Can you see links between these words apart from their spelling patterns?

# Word origins

Many words in the English language have their origins in greek and latin. Although these are both dead languages, they still influence the way we spell today. It can also be helpful to understand the meaning of some root words. For example, the word 'autobiography' is made up of three greek words: auto comes from *autos* meaning self or same; bio comes from *bios* meaning life, and graphy comes from *graphein* meaning to write. So it is easy to work out that an autobiography is a written version of somebody's life written by that person!

## The spelling detective investigates...

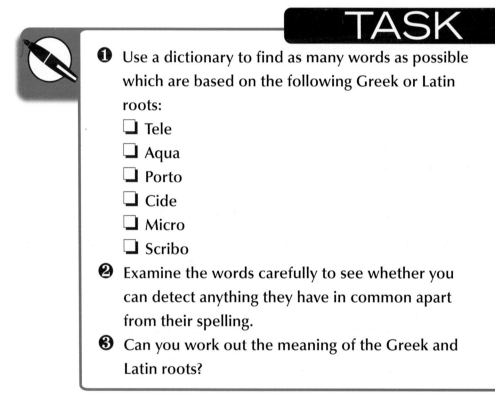

# TASK

❶ Use a dictionary to find as many words as possible which are based on the following Greek or Latin roots:
- ❏ Tele
- ❏ Aqua
- ❏ Porto
- ❏ Cide
- ❏ Micro
- ❏ Scribo

❷ Examine the words carefully to see whether you can detect anything they have in common apart from their spelling.

❸ Can you work out the meaning of the Greek and Latin roots?

# Three top tips

This unit has focused on self-help strategies but there are several rules which may help you.

## The drop rule

Drop a silent 'e' at the end of a word if the new ending begins with a vowel or a 'y'.

Example: hope + ing = hoping
Example: tape + ed = taped

## The swap rule

Swap a 'y' at the end of a word for an 'i' if the 'y' has a consonant in front of it.

Example: happy + ness = happiness

You only break this rule if a double vowel would result, for example, carry + ing cannot become carriing.

When you join two words with an apostrophe, make sure that you put the apostrophe where the letter or letters have been left out and not where the words are joined.

Example: did not = didn't
Example: she will = she'll

# Checking your work

There will be times when you simply need to check the spelling of a word in a dictionary. There are different types of dictionaries available and it is important that you find one that suits your needs. You may wish to use a spelling dictionary which focuses on the spelling of a word. While it will not provide you with extra information about a word, such as its definition, you may find it easier to use if you simply wish to check a spelling.

You will find it easier to use a dictionary quickly and efficiently if you are confident and familiar with the alphabet. If you are not, copy it into your spy notebook for easy reference.

Think about a dictionary divided into four sections or quartiles. The letters in each quartile would be:

First quartile: a–d
Second quartile: e–l
Third quartile: m–r
Fourth quartile: s–z

This should help you to locate a word more easily.

However good a speller you may become, it is always important to proofread your work. However this is not always as easy as it may seem. Sometimes we read what we think we have written and find it difficult to spot our mistakes.

Here are some suggestions which may help:

● Try reading your work backwards, a sentence at a time. This will slow down the reading process and make you more aware of sentence construction
● Work with a partner and proofread each other's work
● Leave your work for a day or two and then check it
● Use a highlighter to mark any spellings which do not look quite right. Focus on the parts of the word which concern you and use a dictionary to check

It is now time to finish sorting out your spelling spy notebook! Its contents could include:

● Spelling strategies which you find useful
● A log of personal errors with corrections
● Your personal spelling lists to learn
● An aide memoire of spelling rules and conventions
● Your findings from spelling investigations
● A list of frequently used words for reference
● Recent spelling attempts
● Key words from different subject areas
● Spelling targets

By combining your own ideas and the ideas from the list, you need to decide on a final list of about ten different sections for your spelling spy notebook. Use page markers to divide your notebook into different sections so that you are able to find your way around it quickly and easily.

You will be able to continue adding to your spy notebook as you continue to revise and consolidate your spelling knowledge.

# UNIT 6 Children or machines?

In this unit you will learn about the following key objectives:

**Stylistic conventions of non-fiction** (persuasive writing) revising the main features of persuasive writing in which you argue powerfully and convincingly in order to make others agree with you

**Stylistic conventions of non-fiction** (discursive writing) revising the main features of discursive writing in which you weigh up more than one point of view before reaching your own conclusion

**Express a view** – using your knowledge and understanding of these two text types to write a persuasive letter to a major sports company as well as working collaboratively on a piece of writing which weighs up the reasons why children should, or should not, have part-time jobs

**KEY OBJECTIVES**

## Child labour: then and now

In 1842 a report on the use of children as workers in the coal mines shocked the Victorian public. The report helped to produce the world's first serious legislation against child labour. However, it was not until 1880, when education for children under ten was made compulsory, that the use of children in dangerous work really began to stop.

Today, children continue to be part of the labour market. In many parts of the world, children continue to work in full-time jobs at a very early age. So what has changed? Why do children work? Should children work?

The Global March Against Child Labour begins in the Philipines.

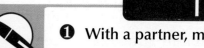

# TASK

❶ With a partner, make a list of three things you already know about child labour.

❷ Read the following extracts. The first was written in 1863 about boy chimney sweeps; the second was written in 1999 about a child who stitches soccer balls in the Punjab.

**g** Brine: salt water

---

## The Water Babies

No one knows the cruelty which a boy has to undergo in learning. The flesh must be hardened. This is done by rubbing it, chiefly on the elbows and knees with the strongest **brine**, as that got from a pork-shop, close by a hot fire. You must stand over them with a cane, or coax them by a promise of a halfpenny, etc. if they will stand a few more rubs.

At first they will come back from their work with their arms and knees streaming with blood, and the knees looking as if the caps had been pulled off. Then they must be rubbed with brine again, and perhaps go off at once to another chimney.

---

## Letter to Tahira Bibi

I doubt I can ever forget you. Your solemn face, your swollen, stitching fingers, your apparent serenity as hour by relentless hour you worked to make soccer balls that, in another place, another world, help make millionaires.

… as the sun goes down and the pesky flies start to leave … your fingers ache with the effort of sewing your third 32-panel ball of the day. For each ball, you get 30 cents, which of course means that somebody is profiting greatly from your labour.

---

# TASK

❶ With a partner, discuss your reactions to these extracts.

❷ The writers of both extracts seem appalled at the conditions in which these children live and work. Find evidence from each extract to support this claim.

❸ Discuss the similarities and differences between the experiences of the children in the two extracts.

Now read the following extract from *The Water Babies* by Charles Kingsley. Kingsley wrote this book for his youngest son in 1863. It tells the story of a young chimney sweep called Tom who runs away from his employer. He falls into a river and is transformed into a water baby.

### The Water Babies

Once upon a time there was a little chimney-sweep, and his name was Tom. That is a short name, and you have heard it before, so you will not have much trouble in remembering it. He lived in a great town in the North country, where there were plenty of chimneys to sweep, and plenty of money for Tom to earn and his master to spend. He could not read nor write, and did not care to do either; and he never washed himself, for there was no water up the court where he lived. He had never been taught to say his prayers. He had never heard of God, or of Christ, except in words which you never have heard, and which it would have been well if he had never heard. He cried half his time, and laughed the other half. He cried when he had to climb the dark **flues**, rubbing his poor knees and elbows raw; and when the soot got into his eyes, which it did every day in the week; and when his master beat him, which he did every day in the week; and when he had not enough to eat, which happened every day in the week likewise. And he laughed the other half of the day, when he was tossing halfpennies with the other boys, or playing leapfrog over the posts, or bowling stones at the horses' legs as they trotted by, which last was excellent fun, when there was a wall at hand behind which to hide. As for chimney-sweeping, and being hungry, and being beaten, he took all that for the way of the world, like the rain and snow and thunder, and stood manfully with his back to it till it was over…

**Flue:** the inside shaft of the chimney which the boys had to climb

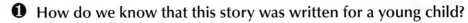

## TASK

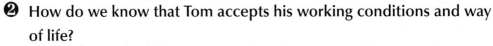

**Work with a partner to explore your responses to the following questions:**

❶ How do we know that this story was written for a young child?

❷ How do we know that Tom accepts his working conditions and way of life?

❸ How do we know that the narrator does not share Tom's view?

❹ Compose one sentence explaining what point you think the writer was making when he wrote this. Share your sentence with the class.

# TASK

Read this account below, written by Pablo – a 14 year-old boy working in Columbia today. As you read, make a note of any similarities and differences between Pablo's experience of child labour and Tom's. Remember that Tom's story was fictional whereas Pablo's is factual.

Think about:

- The different way that this text is presented to us
- The type of work Pablo does
- The physical conditions he suffers
- His feelings
- His secret

## Pablo's Story

Pablo is 14 years old. He lives in a very poor part of Bogota [Colombia's capital city] with his mother and four brothers and sisters. His mother works full time in a coffee factory. His father is a violent alchoholic, who left home a short time ago.

**This is Pablo's story:**

We moved from place to place when I was young.

When I was twelve years old we moved here, to Bogota. A lot of children in my neighbourhood worked as porters and vendors in Bogota's largest street market, so I went along with them. About 200 kids work in the market.

Every day, I get up at 5.30 a.m. It takes nearly two hours to get to the market by bus, and I start work at eight. My work is to unload the trucks which bring the food to the market. I try to unload fruit trucks, because I don't like carrying meat.

The market sellers don't like us to sell fruit because we offer better prices than they do. They throw rotten vegetables at us and they try to chase us away.

Sometimes, the security guards don't allow us to work at all because the law says we are too young. If we try to get into the market, they hit us with sticks until we run away – but it is easy for us to lose the guards and start selling things again. We work in pairs: one kid sells things, while the other kid watches for the men with sticks.

**I have to work**

Although I like my job and I have a lot of friends on the market, I don't choose to work. I work because I must, to help my mother and to pay for my food and so on. I want to go to school. I think my father should pay for my education, so that I don't have to work on the market. I want to be a systems engineer, but how can I?

It's wrong that children have to work, but we do. It is even more wrong that people try to stop us working. If I can, I work all day and finish around seven o'clock in the evening. Afterwards my friends and I play football to relax, but I also have to help clean the house and make dinner, so I don't get much free time.

My life is very tiring, but I enjoy myself. I earn between $5 and $8 per day and I use the money to buy food and clothes.

**Pablo's secret**

Pablo does not tell us about the biggest problem that threatens his future. Pablo's social worker says that Pablo is slowly going blind. If he doesn't have surgery to correct the problem, he will be unable to see by the time he is twenty years old.

## Exploring viewpoints

Many people have strong views both for and against child labour. Their views often depend on how much they benefit from it financially or on how strongly they feel about the humanitarian issues involved.

# TASK

❶ Work in groups of five or six. Each group member should choose one of the following roles:
- ❏ Child worker
- ❏ Parent of child worker
- ❏ Factory owner
- ❏ Journalist from UK
- ❏ UK Sports Company with factories in developing world
- ❏ Oxfam aid worker

❷ Think about the role this person might have in promoting or defending child labour and compose a statement which articulates his or her point of view. When you are ready, rehearse your statement aloud and write it down on your role play card. Listen to each statement in your group.

Example: Parent of child worker 'My child is 12 years old and brings home more money than I do. We need this money to pay for food for my babies.'

❸ Move into a group with others who chose the same role play card as you so that you can collect more statements to bring back to your original group. Write these statements on your card.

❹ Move back to your original group and present two new statements to your group.

❺ Compose one sentence explaining what you have learnt from this activity.

You are now going to read two persuasive texts which are both critical of child labour in other parts of the world. The first is an extract from an article written by Richard Lloyd Parry; the second is adapted from an article commissioned by Christian Aid.

# Nike and Adidas 'have failed to stop sweatshop abuses'

**By Richard Lloyd Parry**

INDONESIAN workers producing sports shoes for the multinational companies Nike and Adidas live in extreme poverty and face prosecution and physical assault for trade union activity, according to a report published yesterday.

Although conditions have improved over the last 18 months, workers are still subjected to verbal abuse, intrusive physical examinations and dangerous conditions.

Timothy Connor, author of the report, *We Are Not Machines*, published in Australia by Oxfam Community Aid Abroad, said: "Nike and Adidas have not done enough to address the concerns of human rights groups, consumers and workers themselves."

"Those improvements which have occurred are commendable, and demonstrate that positive change in response to international pressure is possible. Unfortunately they fall well short of ensuring that Nike and Adidas workers are able to live with dignity," he added.

Nike, the world's largest sports shoe company, has 11 Indonesian factories producing up to 55 million pairs of shoes a year. Only one pair in 50 is sold in Indonesia, the majority being exported to the United States.

The company is paying the golfer Tiger Woods $100m (£70m) for a five-year endorsement contract. But full-time workers at its factories are paid as little as $2 (£1.40) a day. Workers are thus forced to work long hours, and parents with children often have to send them away to be brought up by relatives in other parts of the country, and see them only three or four times a year.

At the Nikomas Gemilang factory in west Java, which produces sports shoes for both Nike and Adidas, half a dozen workers are reported to lose fingers in cutting machinery every year, although there has been a reduction in illnesses caused by poisonous organic solvents used in the process.

"Fear dominates the lives of these workers," the report concludes. "They are afraid that speaking openly about factory conditions or getting involved in active unions will put their livelihoods in danger."

The *Independent*, 8 March 2002

❶ Pick out some of the words and phrases from the text which suggest that the workers are badly treated.

❷ Who does the writer suggest is to blame for their working conditions?

# Revisiting viewpoints

Think back to the work you did with role play cards earlier in the unit. There are many different viewpoints in the article from the *Independent*.

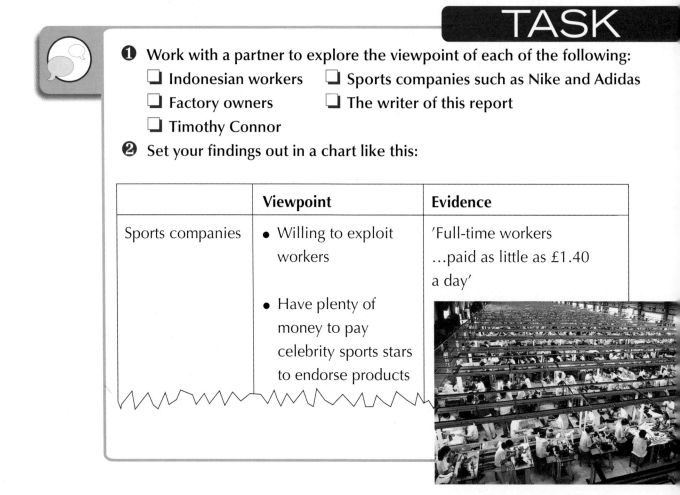

## TASK

❶ Work with a partner to explore the viewpoint of each of the following:
- ❏ Indonesian workers    ❏ Sports companies such as Nike and Adidas
- ❏ Factory owners    ❏ The writer of this report
- ❏ Timothy Connor

❷ Set your findings out in a chart like this:

|  | Viewpoint | Evidence |
|---|---|---|
| Sports companies | • Willing to exploit workers | 'Full-time workers ...paid as little as £1.40 a day' |
|  | • Have plenty of money to pay celebrity sports stars to endorse products | |

# Putting across a point of view

While it helps to have a strong point of view about a controversial issue like child labour, it is also important to be able to present that point of view forcefully. Now read the second text on the next page.

# Globe trotting trainers

HERE'S A GOOD question to wrong-foot your friends. Ask them what companies like Reebok, Nike, Puma, Hi-Tec and Adidas make. When you get the answer 'sports shoes' you can reply 'wrong'.

Sure, these companies are in the sports shoes business. They design the logos for them, they write snappy adverts for them, they pay athletes a fortune to promote them, they market them and sell them. But they do not make them. Why not? For the simple reason that there is no money to be made in manufacturing any more.

Instead, the manufacturing falls to those who have few options. Those who have only their labour to sell have no bargaining power to command a decent wage. They are the world's poor. So for the past 20 years the big name sports shoes companies have simply shopped around the Third World, contracting out production to factories in countries where labour costs are cheapest. In this instance it means the poor in the countries of south-east Asia.

The enormous company Nike, for example, has a workforce of just 8,000 employees. The 75,000 people who make their trainers are employed by subcontractors. These subcontractors are often shared by sports companies. So, if you visited an Asian factory producing the shoes you might see competitors' brands rolling off the production lines side by side.

Aid agency Christian Aid has launched a campaign against the inequalities that the trade produces. It has highlighted the stark contrasts between the hi-tech, high performance glamour of the sports shoes in the UK and the struggle for existence of those who work on the production lines.

'A typical pair of trainers sells for £50 in Britain' says Peter Madden, author of the report *The Globe Trotting Sports Shoe*. 'But the forty or so factory workers in the Philippines who make the trainers will share just over £1 of that price between them'.

Christian Aid charges the sports shoes companies with shortchanging the workers in Asia. It has calculated how long it would take a young production worker to earn the annual salary of Nike boss Phil Knight. On current wages a young woman in China would have to work nine hours a day, six days a week, for fifteen centuries to match his 1994 pay of £929,113.

The charity acknowledges that shoe manufacturing generates valuable jobs and money for Third World countries, but claims that wages and working conditions are unsatisfactory. It points to abuses such as enforced overtime, health and safety deficiencies, discrimination against trade unions, and hire-and-fire policies that avoid payment of fringe benefits. If workers in a country begin to organise, demand basic employment rights and increased wages, the companies can simply switch their place of production – even to another country.

Christian Aid is urging supporters to write to the five companies asking them to pay higher wages and improve factory conditions.

*Young People Now*, March 1996

## TASK

Re-read the article 'Globe trotting trainers', looking closely at the way the ideas are organised. The following prompts might help you:

- The impact of the opening paragraph on the reader
- The way each paragraph introduces and develops a new idea
- The way each paragraph has a topic sentence which is expanded upon in the rest of the paragraph
- The way the final paragraph calls for action

# How to persuade – working on sentences

Now that you have identified many of the issues and points of view surrounding child labour, you are going to explore how opinions on these issues can be shaped by language. You will soon become an expert in manipulating words and sentences to persuade somebody else that your viewpoint is the one that counts!

Remember: a simple sentence contains one main clause. Look at this simple sentence:

*Some children have to work hard.*

Is this a good opening sentence for a piece of writing to persuade people to think again about dangerous child labour in other parts of the world?

How could it be improved? You could write:

> 'Labour' is a stronger verb than 'work' in this context

*Millions of small children have to labour in dangerous conditions.*

> Notice how a number is substituted to add much more impact

> The adjective 'small' is emotive and likely to make your reader feel pity. The adjective 'dangerous' is likely to make them feel concern

> The noun 'conditions' implies a lot more about the environment

## TASK

Look at the following two simple sentences and try to make them more persuasive by using some of the techniques in the example above.

❶ The workers are afraid of the factory owners.
❷ Some children lose limbs in the factories.

You might:
- Change a noun to add specific detail
- Add strong or emotive adjectives to describe nouns
- Use numbers or phrases containing numbers for factual impact
- Try to make main verbs stronger

Simple sentences, containing one main idea, can also be turned into compound sentences where two or more ideas are linked using 'and' or 'but'. Compound sentences contain two or more main clauses which have equal importance.

*Millions of small children have to labour in dangerous conditions __and__ they can suffer terrible consequences.*

Notice how the conjunction 'and' allows the writer to include another idea. A conjunction is rather like a small hinge allowing you to link ideas together.

Other conjunctions such as: as, as if, because, before, if, that, though, until, unless, whenever, where, while and whose can also be used to link two or more ideas to give an even better picture and to make the reader feel a particular response. By linking clauses with these conjunctions you can create complex sentences.

*Millions of small children labour in hazardous conditions __where__ their health, their education and even their lives are put at risk.*

This has now become a complex sentence because the subordinate clause provides extra layers of detail. The use of 'where' rather than 'and' allows the writer to describe the conditions of work more vividly.

Notice that the adjective 'dangerous' has been replaced with 'hazardous' for even more dramatic effect.

You may also notice that the writer has listed *three* ways in which child labour can have negative impact – 'their health', 'their education' and 'their lives'. Groups of three words or phrases are often used in persuasive writing. This is known as a pattern of three and is often found in persuasive speeches.

## TASK

Look back at one of your simple sentences and see if you can turn it into a compound or a complex sentence. Read it out to your partner and gauge its impact.

# A letter to Nike

## Preparing your letter

You are now going to begin to plan a letter to a major sports company on the subject of child labour in the developing world. Your aim is to highlight all the issues surrounding developing world labour and the use of children in the workforce. You will then persuade the company to improve conditions for the workers and ban child labour in their factories.

The following statements will remind you of some of the viewpoints you have encountered in this unit so far:

The workers are lucky…I don't think the workers in our factories are badly treated. The wages may be small, but it's better than having no job.
Nike

It's not our business. I don't think it's something you can lay at a shoe company and say 'You must accept responsibility for improving the social and living conditions of all employees'.
Adidas

A typical pair of trainers sells for £50 in Britain. The forty or so factory workers in the Philippines who make the trainers will share just over £1 of that price between them.
Peter Madden, author of *The Globe Trotting Sports Shoe*

On current wages a young woman in China would have to work nine hours a day, six days a week, for fifteen centuries to match Nike boss, Phil Knight's salary of £929,113.
'Globe Trotting Trainers', *Young People Now*, Christian Aid

## Planning your letter in six easy steps

Before you begin, remind yourself of the way the writer organised his ideas in the persuasive article 'Globe Trotting Trainers' on page 117.

### Step one

Decide on five or six main ideas for your letter.

### Step two

Place each idea at the top of a post-it note and stick it on your desk.

### Step three

Move the post-it notes around until you are happy with the order of ideas. Each post-it note will represent a paragraph.

### Step four

Now, compose a strong topic sentence for the first paragraph. Write this on the post-it note.

Discuss your first sentence with a partner. Is it clear? Does it give the reader a clear indication of your point of view?

### Step five

Construct a topic sentence for each of your other paragraphs and write these on the remaining post-it notes. Think about the last post-it note very carefully.

### Step six

You are now ready to collect your thoughts and ideas for your letter. Mark each post-it note with a colour or symbol. Read back through the work you have done on child labour so far. Use the colours/symbols to mark relevant points that could go under each section of your letter. Jot down these supporting ideas on your post-it note or next to each post-it note in your exercise book.

# Writing your letter

When you are ready, begin writing your first paragraph. As you write, think about using the persuasive devices you have learned about and try to vary your sentences. Remember to use:

- Powerful or emotive adjectives
- Repetition of key words and phrases
- Exaggerated use of language
- Strong contrasts
- Rhetorical questions
- Use of personal pronouns: I, you, we
- Patterns of three
- Dramatic use of numbers

## Hot tips!

- Re-read your work aloud as you compose each new sentence
- When you have completed your first paragraph, check that each sentence is connected to the main idea on your post-it note
- When you are ready, move on to the second paragraph and so on until you have completed a first draft of your letter. Repeat the check after you complete each paragraph of the letter
- Make sure that your final paragraph leaves the reader with a clear idea of what must be done

# Drafting, editing and proofreading

## TASK

Work in pairs to edit each other's work. Look for:

- Ideas which are logically organised
- An introduction which draws the reader in
- A powerful conclusion with a demand for action
- A variety of sentences – simple, compound and complex
- Persuasive language features like those listed on page 122
- Careful punctuation

## Example

### Before redrafting

*Your company must act soon and you should improve working conditions. We should create jobs for developing countries, but it is wrong that you treat these people differently. Just because you can spend money on big adverts and influence young people to buy expensive gear, doesn't mean we don't know what is going on in these factories. If you don't do something soon, no one will want the shame of wearing your products in public.*

This compound sentence has been developed into a complex sentence. The colon allows the writer to state specifically what he/she wants the companies to do. Why is the first part of the sentence now more urgent?

A good second sentence but how could you summarise exactly what is wrong? Could you add a pattern of three?

A strong way to finish. Words like 'shame', 'you', 'your' make the reader feel guilt. The last sentence carries a warning which works well. What could be done with words like 'gear' and 'big'? Where else could words or phrases be more precise?

### After redrafting

*There is now only one course of action for top shoe manufacturers to take: to improve working conditions and increase wages. We should create jobs for developing countries but enforced overtime, poverty and child labour must not continue. Until companies like yours, who spend millions on attracting young customers, listen to our opinions, we will look at your products with disgust. Act now.*

Another way of phrasing a similar idea. Look how the last two sentences are very different in length. The first is complex, containing a range of important ideas and emotive language. The last is a simple command.

So what has changed since the days of the chimney-sweep? Is childhood a time of innocence, play and freedom from responsibilities? Or is there a place for children in the labour market? So far, you have concentrated on one side of an argument. In the final part of this unit, you will learn how to weigh up more than one point of view.

# TASK

You are going to read a discursive essay on child labour called 'Is Child Labour Wrong?' Discursive writing tends to consider more than one angle of an issue. Rather than aiming to persuade, this writer considers several views of child labour and reaches her own conclusion.

Read the article very carefully and think about how it is different from the texts you studied earlier in this unit.

## Is child labour wrong?

Many people believe that childhood should be a time of innocence and a time of freedom from pressures of adult life. These people campaign strongly against what they regard as the exploitation of young people today. However, children continue to work throughout the world, as they always have done. The issues are complex.

It is not difficult to understand why people feel so strongly about the exploitation of children. One has only to read accounts of young people working for a pittance in developing world sweatshops to feel disgust and outrage at their treatment. Many work up to sixteen hours a day for seven days a week. Their working conditions are appalling and they are paid next to nothing for their work. Children stitch footballs for pennies and yet the footballers earn thousands of pounds a week! This hardly seems fair!

Many people argue that childhood should be a time for children to play and learn. Childhood is the time for young people to gain a good education which will improve their life chances. How is this possible when they are working such long hours? Without a good education, how will they ever raise themselves out of the poverty in which they live?

*continued*

However, children have always worked and continue to do so. In peasant societies children have always taken part in the working life of the family, both in agriculture and domestic tasks. In the large labouring populations of Thailand, Indonesia and China, every available worker is crucial to the economy, including children. For many families, it is vital that their children are put to work as soon as they are able. Many families in the developing world depend on their children for survival. If their children don't work, the family will starve!

The debate seems to be centred around the definition of childhood. Is childhood a time of innocence, play and freedom from responsibility or is it a period where children learn skills that make them employable? The answer largely depends on where you live and on your own experience of work and education. In Bangladesh, you will not find many people who hold the first view. Training children in the skills needed to earn a living wage is regarded as much more important. The idea that childhood should be a time of imagination and play is a fairly modern idea.

Perhaps the most important concern is not whether children work or not but whether they have access to education. Campaigns against the abuse of children in Victorian England may have started in the early 1800s but it was not until 1880, when education was made compulsory for children under ten that things  began to change. Perhaps what is needed is a balanced view of childhood which prioritises education but allows different cultures to place their own value on work?

① Provide a title for each of the six paragraphs.

② What do you notice about the way the ideas are organised?

③ Complete the following chart to show the main differences between persuasive and discursive writing:

| Persuasive writing | Discursive writing |
| --- | --- |
| Gives one side of an argument | Weighs up more than one side of an argument |

You are now going to compose a piece of discursive writing with your class. The title of the piece is 'Should school children have part-time jobs?' The essay will contain a range of different views and reflections including your personal thoughts.

There are six key paragraphs. The topic sentence for each paragraph is presented opposite. You will notice that in this essay each argument is followed by a counter-argument, and then by a final conclusion.

Collecting together your thoughts from the last few weeks, work in pairs to complete each paragraph. Person A should work on completing paragraphs 2 and 4. Person B can work on completing paragraphs 3 and 5. You should compose the introduction and the conclusion together. Read your arguments and counter-arguments back to each other as you write.

# Should school children have part-time jobs?

## Introduction
Many children have part-time jobs while still at school...

However, some people feel that ...

## Paragraph 2
Part-time employment can provide many young people with valuable experience.

## Paragraph 3
On the other hand, students who have jobs might find it difficult to keep up with their school work.

## Paragraph 4
Many students like to earn money of their own.

## Paragraph 5
However, many would argue that parents should support their children financially while they are in full-time education.

## Conclusion
In conclusion, ...

During this unit you have learned about the important conventions of **persuasive** and **discursive** writing. Look out for some of these conventions when you read newspapers, magazines and other non-fiction texts on important world issues. When you come to write your own persuasive or discursive texts, the following key points are worth remembering:

**In persuasive writing:**

- Build noun phrases by using powerful or emotive adjectives
- Repeat key words and phrases
- Make strong contrasts
- Use rhetorical questions
- Use personal pronouns: I, you, we
- Make patterns of three
- Vary sentences

**In discursive writing:**

- Use the third person and past tense when you are giving a historical picture
- Use the first person and present tense when you express a view
- Keep your introduction balanced – don't indicate your opinion
- Arrange paragraphs in a sequence to balance two or more sides of an argument
- Use evidence to support your arguments
- Use key topic sentences to direct your reader
- Use the conclusion to indicate your final position

# UNIT 7 It's showtime!

In this unit you will learn about the following key objectives:

**Collaborate on scripts** – working together to investigate the structure of plays and the ways characters and situations are introduced

**Present findings** – interpreting a selection of extracts and dramatising your own scripts and those of other playwrights

You will be asked to read a variety of playscripts so that you understand how they are put together and how you might respond as a member of an audience. These insights will help you to interpret extracts from plays. Later in the unit you will devise and present your interpretations of scenes from plays, some by recognised playwrights, others devised by you.

As you work through the unit, you will keep a journal of your insights and ideas. Many playwrights jot down ideas for scenes or characters to help them clarify their thinking. Your journal will enable you to clarify your own ideas as you work within a group to present your dramas.

# It's showtime!

We all love watching plays but they are not only performed on stage. Plays also appear on television but they are often performed without a live audience. They can still be called 'plays' because they have a common structure. They have a beginning which is called an 'exposition', a development, a crisis and a conclusion which is called a 'denouement'.

## TASK

Working in groups, make a list of plays you can remember watching on the stage or on television. Which are your favourites? Why?

One of the hardest things to do is to start writing a play when you have not formed your ideas for the plot properly. Often writers use one of the following techniques to get their ideas flowing:

- **Start with a theme.** For example, war, religion, power, sport or school
- **Choose a crisis.** For example, a person being lost, a fire or an accident
- **Think about a location.** For example, a hospital, a haunted house or a sleepy country village
- **Adapt an existing story.** For example, ideas may come from songs, books or newspaper stories. Shakespeare's idea for *Romeo and Juliet* was from a poem

## TASK

Working in pairs, brainstorm ideas for your own play. Think about the theme you want to develop and then consider the following:
- How would you begin your play?
- Where would you locate the action?
- How would you develop the characters and themes?
- What would be the crisis?
- How would you conclude your play?

You are now going to use improvisation to make your ideas come alive!

Improvisation is a technique where you work from a given set of circumstances. For instance, two people are sitting on a bus which has broken down. From this point you make up the action and dialogue. It might go something like this:

"Now we get to make it up"

"Not so fast. We have to remember to stay in role and think like our characters do".

| | |
|---|---|
| **Driver:** | Sorry, but the engine's packed in. |
| **Passenger:** | But I'm due at a meeting in 20 minutes. |
| **Driver:** | Well, I'm afraid you'll have to walk. |
| **Passenger:** | Walk! It's at least 3 miles! You have to do something! |

Improvisation is great fun because you have to think on your feet and react to what other characters may say to you. Improvisation also helps you to understand the situation you have devised.

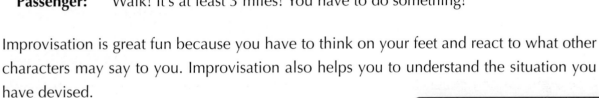

# TASK

❶ You have already created a plot to improvise and develop in your brainstorming activity. You now need an opening line for your improvisation. Either choose from the suggestions below or make up your own.
   ❑ Can you keep a secret?
   ❑ I've got a dreadful pain in my stomach.
   ❑ Quick! Call the fire brigade.
   ❑ Do you like him?
   ❑ I've lost my ring.

*Log Sheet 1*

*Improvisation*

*Today I improvised.*

*I made the following decisions ...*

*Improvisation helped me to ...*

❷ Working in pairs at your desks, improvise one of these situations. Remember, you should work together to keep the improvisation going. How long can you stay in role?

❸ Using your journal, jot down a brief outline of your improvisation. Record what happened, the quick decisions you were forced to make and what you found difficult. Do you think your improvisation was successful? How could you have developed it?

## Clues about characters

Characters are essential elements of plays. A playwright needs to think carefully about the characters, their views and behaviours and how they react to one another. You are going to explore an existing character to see what makes him/her tick. You will build up your understanding of the character from snippets of information. In other words, you are going to **deduce** your understanding.

# TASK

One picture shows Brian as a baby. What clues can we deduce about him at this early age? What do you think the picture suggests about him?

# TASK

❶ This is Brian at 10 years old. What clues do we have about him now? Think carefully about his appearance and mood.

❷ Read the following short extract from 'The Short History of Brian Beck' by Ray Robinson.

## The Short History of Brian Beck

**Mother:** You really must learn to look after your things, Brian.

Just look at your shoes! You've been playing football in them again.

**Anne:** Just look at your shirt collar, Brian! You've been fighting again, haven't you?

**Mary:** You've been down that pond again, haven't you?

Look at the mud on those socks!

**Susan:** Just look at the state of those trousers! You've been playing on that rubbish dump again, haven't you?

**Narrator:** And he had, of course. Played football. Fought. Fished for sticklebacks. Looked in the rubbish dump for gold rings. And started a huge collection of –

**John:** Cigarette packets.

**Graham:** Bus numbers.

**David:** Pictures of Manchester United.

**Angela:** Stamps from all over the world, but mainly from England.

**Jennifer:** Bus tickets that he put in a tin and swapped for a model aeroplane which never flew.

**Narrator:** He got tonsillitis. And appendicitis. And toothache. And earache. And trouble at school. Trouble at school was the worst thing he ever got. There was a new teacher called Mr Barrett. Mr Barrett hated litter, and all forms of untidiness.

**Mr Barrett:** You're ten years old, Brian Beck, and you sit there dropping paper on the floor. Look at the mess!

………….

**Narrator:** Brian found it hard to get anything right. His sums went wrong. And his spellings. And his writing. And even his pictures.

**Mr Barrett:** Just look at this disgraceful mess. All this paint and water. What a disgusting mess, lad!

**Brian:** Sorry, sir.

**Mr Barrett:** Being sorry's no good, lad, if you don't try to make things better.

**Brian:** No, sir. Sorry, sir.

**Narrator:** And Brian even came to hate Mr Barrett. He had never hated anyone in all his life before. But Mr Barrett was making school terrible for him. Brian lay in bed at night wondering how he could possibly get free from Mr Barrett.

# TASK

❶ You are now going to hot seat Brian in order to gain more information about his life. Prepare three questions you would like to ask him. Then, choose a volunteer, place him or her on the hot seat and see what else you can learn about Brian Beck.

❷ Using your journal, write down what you have found out about Brian by hot seating him.

❶ Working in groups of four, discuss how the writer informs the audience about Brian.

❷ Test your understanding of Brian's character. Discuss how Brian would act and feel in a different setting, perhaps at school, and then feedback to the whole group.

❸ Create a character for your own play which fits in with the plans you have already made. Make notes in your journal about the character's appearance, mood, relationships with friends and family, talents and anything else you think is important.

## Selling drama

The climax of a play is often the most challenging to write as it has to be packed with pace and drama. It is the part of the play which needs both tension and excitement.

You are going to become specialists working in four groups. Each group will have a different focus looking at four different aspects of a play entitled 'Julian'.

**Group A**

You will look at how punctuation makes the extract dramatic.

**Group B**

You will look at the stage directions in brackets. What do we learn about action and characters when we read the stage directions?

**Group C**

You will look at the language used. Which words and phrases tell us most about Julian? What sort of a character is he?

**Group D**

You will focus on the tension. Which section is the most tense? Why is this? Do any of the stage directions make parts of the scene more tense? Why?

# *Julian*

| | |
|---|---|
| JULIAN | (Mocking) Silence in court! Your name? |
| FINCH | Father Christmas! |
| JULIAN | You're on trial kid, name? |
| FINCH | Finch. |
| JULIAN | Christian name? |
| FINCH | What do you want to know that for? |
| JULIAN | Christian name? (Pause) Christian name? |
| FINCH | Timothy. |

(Sniggers from group)

| | |
|---|---|
| DAVE | (Unbelieving) Timothy!!! |
| FINCH | I'll fill you lot in! |

(The laughter stops abruptly)

| | |
|---|---|
| JULIAN | Sit down – Timofy. |

(Silence)

| | |
|---|---|
| JULIAN | Right, Timofy – |
| FINCH | Shut up! |
| JULIAN | But it's your name! I always call my friends by their first name – don't I Gordon? |
| GORDON | Yes, Julian. |
| FINCH | I ain't your friend, girly! |
| JULIAN | But you're still called Timofy. |
| FINCH | Get on with it! |
| SANDRA | I'm cold! |
| JULIAN | You aren't afraid of anything Finch, Timofy? |
| FINCH | No. |
| JULIAN | Nothing? |
| FINCH | No. |
| JULIAN | Anything I ask you to do – you'll do? |
| FINCH | I said so, ain't I! |

(Steps)

| | |
|---|---|
| JULIAN | (Gently) Can I have it a minute? |
| ALLY | He's all asleep. |
| JULIAN | Only a minute. |
| ALLY | Alright. |

(Steps…and stop.)

| | |
|---|---|
| JULIAN | (Gently) See this? |
| FINCH | Yes. |
| JULIAN | What is it? |
| FINCH | A tortoise – blind are you! |
| JULIAN | Kill it. |

(Shocked silence)

| | |
|---|---|
| FINCH | What! |
| JULIAN | Cut its head off. Timofy. |

(Silence)

| | |
|---|---|
| FINCH | (Horrified) I – I can't! |
| JULIAN | Scared? |

(Silence)

| | |
|---|---|
| FINCH | Yeah! It's alive! |
| ALLY | No! I want it! You can't touch it! Give it me! |
| JULIAN | Take her away Dave! |

(Ally is crying)

| | |
|---|---|
| DAVE | (scared) Come on, titchy. |
| ALLY | I'm going home! No, I want my tortoise. |

(Silence)

| | |
|---|---|
| SANDRA | You can't do that! |
| JULIAN | Finch can't. |
| SANDRA | You're …you're mad! |
| JULIAN | Ti-mo-fy? |

(Pause)

Not afraid of anything?

(Pause)

Nothing?

(Pause)

Only a little tortoise.

| | |
|---|---|
| FINCH | Give us it then. |
| JULIAN | Presenting one…tiny…baby…tortoise. |

(Silence)

Go on.

| | |
|---|---|
| SANDRA | Don't Finch |

(Silence)

| | |
|---|---|
| FINCH | Ally. Here y'are. |
| ALLY | It's mine! I'm going home! (Runs out) |
| JULIAN | Finch, You're a dead loss – what are you? |
| FINCH | A dead loss. |

## TASK

As a class you are going to take on the roles of buyers and sellers at an imaginary market place. You will be buying and selling information.

❶ Choose a member of your group to stay and 'exchange' the three main points in your journal about 'Julian' for other people's main points.

❷ The rest of you need to shop around the market place exchanging information from other stalls.

❸ The shoppers should feedback to their groups.

## TASK

Record all the gathered information in your journal.

# Which direction?

Stage directions are very important because they give clues to an actor. They explain how an actor should say lines, behave and move. Stage directions also reveal the reactions of other characters and sometimes describe the setting and atmosphere of a scene.

## TASK

Working as a pair, imagine you are actors who have just received the following script by Arthur Miller from your director. However, it does not appear to have any stage directions to help you bring the script to life. Add your own stage directions to impress your director ready for the first rehearsal.

- When would you make the actors pause?
- At what point would you make them angry or fearful?

You are in charge. Direct the actors the way you want the characters to be seen.

**In a shocked, concerned voice**

## Death of a Salesman

**With his hand raised, calming her down**

| | |
|---|---|
| LINDA | Willy! |
| WILLY | It's all right. I came back. |
| LINDA | Why? What happened? Did something happen, Willy? |
| WILLY | No, nothing happened. |
| LINDA | You didn't smash the car, did you? |
| WILLY | I said nothing happened. Didn't you hear me? |
| LINDA | Don't you feel well? |
| WILLY | I'm tired to the death. I couldn't make it. I just couldn't make it. I just couldn't make it, Linda. |
| LINDA | Where were you all day? You look terrible. |
| WILLY | I got as far as a little above Yonkers. I stopped for a cup of coffee. Maybe it was the coffee. |
| LINDA | What? |
| WILLY | I suddenly couldn't drive any more. The car kept going off on to the shoulder, y'know? |
| LINDA | Oh. Maybe it was the steering again, I don't think Angelo knows the Studebaker. |
| WILLY | No, it's me, it's me. Suddenly I realize I'm goin' sixty miles an hour and I don't remember the last five minutes. I'm – I can't seem to – keep my mind to it. |
| LINDA | Maybe its your glasses. You never went for your new glasses. |

## TASK

In your journal, briefly jot down three stage directions you included and give your reasons.

You are now going to adapt a key moment from the prose version of 'The Three Little Pigs' into a TV playscript. This is sometimes called **media transfer** because you are changing the writing from one medium, the novel, into another, a playscript. It is a powerful way of understanding how different texts work.

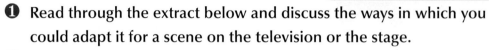

❶ Read through the extract below and discuss the ways in which you could adapt it for a scene on the television or the stage.

❷ Consider which pieces of text should become dialogue and which should become stage directions.

❸ What would you put in as sound effects (abbreviated to 'fx' in scripts)?

## The Three Little Pigs

The little pig who lived in the brick house stopped suddenly and listened. He could clearly hear the sound of trotters galloping towards his door and something else … something more sinister!

In an instant, the front door burst open, and tumbling over the step came his two brothers, flustered and panic-stricken.

'What's wrong?' he cried.

Before any reply came, the door was slammed shut and the large metallic bolts rattled into place. Not before time because, as the two little pigs slumped to the floor, there came a gentle but ominous knocking.

A deep growl came from beyond the old wooden door. 'Let me in, let me in, little pigs or I'll huff and I'll puff and I'll blow your house down!'

The three pigs huddled together trembling at the awful prospect. 'Not by the hair on our chinny, chin, chin!' they finally managed to squeak.

Unable to utter another sound, they nonetheless plucked up the courage to scribble a note to push under the door. It read,

*Dear Mr Wolf,*

*Despite the fact that you have demolished two houses in your rampage through the countryside, your capacity to undermine the foundations of this dwelling will be severely curtailed.*

*Therefore, we have no intention whatsoever of opening the door to you. We believe that you intend to do us personal harm and, on that basis, we respectively suggest that you desist from this behaviour and leave the neighbourhood immediately.*

*Failure to comply will force us to contact the relevant authorities.*

*Yours sincerely,*

*The Three Little Pigs*

From outside the brick house, there came the sound of breath being drawn in …

## TASK

In your journal, write down the changes you needed to make to the Three Little Pigs extract to make it into a TV playscript. Add your reasons.

## Making a scene

## TASK

❶ It is time for you to put pen to paper and write your own scene using both the situation and the character you have already created in your journal. Remember to consider style of speech, punctuation, stage directions and language.

❷ Choose a line you like from your script. Read it out to the class telling them what style of speech you have used and why.

# Writer's Forum

Writers often try their work out on a sample audience to see if their scripts are effective. By doing this, they gain advice on how their scripts could be enhanced and developed.

You are going to use a technique called 'Forum Theatre' which is a convention used by performers who act out a drama while observers watch. Either the performers or the observers can stop the action at any point to offer advice or to add a supportive comment.

## TASK

Choose one script to act out. The whole class should watch, remembering to stop the action where necessary and add a comment to develop the drama. When using Forum Theatre, the emphasis should be on supporting the people in role as they experiment with a range of different ideas. All the suggestions should be supportive.

## TASK

Working in small groups, try out your scripts on each other. Make a note of any changes to your script, and your reasons, in your journal.

## TASK

An interesting way of working on scripts is to interpret the work of other people.
❶ Swap your script with a person from another group and act it out.
❷ Observers and performers should write a comment on the bottom of the script pointing out the positive features and suggesting one way in which it might be improved.

## Editing suite

All writers have their drafts checked by editors before they are published. An editor reads through the script and searches for any errors and problems. This ensures that a script is error free.

**TASK**

You are going to act as editors for each other's scripts. Check through to see if the following criteria have been met:
- Are there clear examples of characterisation?
- Have appropriate choices of language been made?
- Is punctuation used for dramatic effect?
- Did the plot and structure make an impact?
- Were stage directions used clearly to assist the actors?

**TASK**

Now you have finished editing you need to discuss your thoughts about the script with the writer.

**TASK**

In your journal, note any changes made to your script and how they will improve your writing.

## Self review of script writing

One of the best ways to improve your writing is to consider how you might improve it next time. Before you become a critic of other people's scripts, reflect on what you have written yourself.

**TASK**

Read the example below and use it as a guide to help you complete your own review.

| During the process of writing this script I have… | My comments |
|---|---|
| Understood how to create a character | I think my character was interesting because she would do unexpected things and this shocked the audience |
| Created an interesting plot | I am looking forward to the audience reaction. I think they will find my play exciting |
| Understood the structure of a play | I have tried to include the basic stages of a play |
| Used stage directions for effect | Some of my stage directions work really well because I can see in my own mind what I want to happen |
| Considered how characters' actions create drama | It was interesting trying to get the characters moving and reacting as I thought they should |
| Considered the type of English used | Some of my characters needed to use colloquial English because it made them sound more real |
| Shared ideas with other pupils | We all worked together really hard but we didn't always agree |
| Directed and enhanced other people's work | I tried to do this but I found it difficult to think of things to say straight away |
| Edited work and made changes | This worked well because people kept giving me ideas |
| Written a review for a play | This is my next task and I need to think how to suggest things without upsetting people |

### Target
Be more adventurous with my scripts and clearer about the way I write stage directions.

### How I will achieve this
Take more time to think about each step in the scene.

### Support I will need
Other people to listen to my ideas and suggest improvements.

### Date I will have achieved this by
By the end of this term.

# Press night

You've done it! Tonight is going to be a press night, when journalists are invited to come and review your play.

❶ Choose a class member who is not in your play to act as reviewer.

❷ Act out your revised play for your expert audience.

You are about to write reviews for each other's plays. Remember to be as positive as possible. Before you begin, complete the task about reviewing plays on the next page so that you have a clearer idea of the style.

## TASK

Read the review on this page and notice the specific features that you should include in your version.

Opening paragraph gives the reader crucial information – the 'who, what and why' questions are answered.

For variety and formality, sentecnes often start with a subordinate clause.

Characters, and their place in the plot, are quickly introduced.

Punctuation is used for emphasis and effect.

The commentary moves from a summary of the plot to an overall opinion.

There is a clear conclusion to the article.

Unperformed since it was first seen back in 1981, Richard Solley's comic play 'A fortnight in Welles', provides the perfect entertainment for all theatre lovers.

Raised by the kindly but doddering Sir Edward Michael, Lady Hillary Phillips and Lord Andrew Wells have married each other only because the old man planned the match since their birth. Hillary's would-be suitor, Clive Simpson, attempts to woo her in true comic fashion by singing endless ballads outside her apartment wearing ribboned socks! After a period of confusion, Lady Hillary surprises all by agreeing to elope to Welles in a campavan, to escape both. She shockingly reveals the identity of her true love as Roy Thompson, the Butler!

This is an immensely fun production with an impressive cast and set to match. Philomena Durkin, who plays Hillary gives a delightful performance oozing style. Richard Baker looks the perfect comic fool as he parades his stupidity with ease and magical timing.

A final mention must be given to Lynn Foster's exciting and innovative direction making this an evening where you will be left exhausted from laughter.

Jacqueline Hazard

# TASK

❶ Working together as a pair or small group, complete this cloze exercise. It will give you an understanding of the type of words used in theatre reviews. Decide which words you would use to fill in the blanks.

❷ When you have finished, begin planning your own review.

---

## *Shakespeare's summer delight*

### By Joanna Wilson, Victoria Lindrea and Leigh Mytton

### Romeo and Juliet at Regent's Park open air theatre

The drab ____ skies and odd spot of _____ did not prevent the audience from enjoying this jaunty, _____ production.

Set in the 1950s, it was slicked _____ hair and tailored suits for Romeo (Alan Westaway) and friends and _____ outfits for their female counterparts.

There is no doubting that the _____looking Laura Main captured Juliet's naïve innocence. But occasionally, this was marred by her being just a little ____ giggly and girly.

Combined with Romeo's swaggeringly _____ manner, it sometimes made the more serious outpourings of teen angst, passion and grief rather _____.

But whilst the audience was _____ in a haze of frivolity, the _____ turn of events seemed to _____ out of nowhere, instead of gradually escalating out of control.

Of the other cast members, John Hodgkinson and Benedict Cumberbatch are particularly worthy of _____, Hodgkinson as the lively Mercutio whilst Cumberbatch's thoughtful Benvolio was a ___ to watch throughout.

26 June, 2002

# Supportive Critics

When you write a review of a school production, you need to adapt it to for the audience and purpose.

## TASK

Read these two extracts and notice how they have been given a specific purpose and audience.

## St Patrick's English Department Newsletter

There were some fine performances of original scripts this week in Year 7 English groups at St Patrick's. Pupils had gone to great lengths to carefully organise and shape their scripts and this resulted in some exciting and thought-provoking presentations.

In fact, some of the pupils had gone to great lengths to create an authentic atmosphere for their audience by using props and costumes. This enthusiasm clearly had an effect on the audience because their response to the characters and their situations was extremely positive.

No doubt some of these young people will one day 'tread the boards' if they continue their rapid development with scripts and dramatic presentations.

Ms Rashid

## The Dene School Newspaper

**By pupils for pupils!**

The English Department's gone manic this week. There's kids and costumes everywhere! This column has heard that the Year 7 pupils have been hard at work writing, editing and presenting their own scripts and, judging by the reaction of other classes, it's been a real success.

Apparently, some of them even managed to get their teacher to video the presentations so they could watch it all over again next lesson! Wasn't like that when we were in Year 7!

Editor

## TASK

Now it is time to write your own review of the presentations you have seen.

Your work will be assessed in a number of ways throughout Key Stage 3. For example:

✓ Your teacher might talk to you about your work and suggest ways in which you might improve it

✓ You might be asked to work with a partner to make constructive comments about each other's drafted work

✓ You might be asked as a class to comment on a group presentation given by members of your class

✓ You might be set a test which will be marked by your teacher

✓ You might be asked to record some of your recent spelling errors and then think of strategies to learn those words which you find difficult

✓ Your teacher might write a comment at the end of a piece of work that you have done

It is very important, however, that you are fully involved in your own learning. You need to think about your strengths as a reader, writer and speaker and listener. You also need to think about areas which you need to improve. You need to be involved in the process of setting targets which will help you and your teacher to enable you to make progress in certain areas. This unit focuses on this process.

# Myself as a reader

I've read all of the Harry Potter books and I've seen the films. I enjoyed the books more because I was able to imagine what the characters looked like

My favourite book is Harry Potter and the Prisoner of Azkaban by J.K. Rowling

My other favourite authors are Philip Pullman and Michael Morpurgo

If I find a book I like, I often read other books written by the same writer

I especially like reading stories which keep me guessing until the very end

I buy a computer magazine every month

Sometimes I swap books with my friends

I sometimes borrow books from the school library but I don't belong to a local library

I might read a newspaper at home — usually the sports pages

I often go on the internet at home

My friends often send me text messages which I enjoy reading

I got a mobile phone for my birthday and had to read the booklet of instructions to work out how to use it

# TASK

Make a mind map for yourself like the one opposite.
Then draw out your strengths as a reader as well as
the areas you would like to develop. The following
ideas might help you:

**What I think I'm good at**
- I read a lot of fiction
- I talk about books with my friends
- I make pictures in my mind of people and
  places I read about

**Three things I'd like to improve about my reading**
1   I'd like to read more non-fiction
2   I'd like to read books by other writers rather
    than the same ones all the time
3   I'd like to be better at skimming and scanning –
    I tend to read quite slowly and don't always
    think about why I am reading

**My reading targets**
- To read three novels by the end of term which
  are written by writers whose work I haven't
  read before
- To practise using skimming and scanning as
  reading strategies to find information for my
  History project

I enjoy writing stories and I think I'm quite good at building suspense. My friends enjoy reading my stories

I often get ideas for my writing from books I have read

I don't always bother to plan my work – I prefer just to start writing when I get an idea

My handwriting is a little bit untidy – I prefer to use a computer

My spelling is quite good; if I don't know how to spell a word I try to work it out

I'm never quite sure when to start a new paragraph

I don't always remember to check my writing after I've finished

I can use quite a lot of punctuation but I often forget to put full stops into my writing. Speech marks are a bit tricky too

I don't really enjoy writing non-fiction although I quite enjoyed writing a persuasive letter recently

I enjoy playing around with sentences – I can move a subordinate clause around a sentence and I can start a sentence in different ways

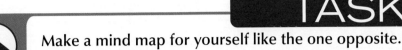

Make a mind map for yourself like the one opposite. Then draw out your strengths as a writer as well as the areas you would like to develop. The following ideas might help you:

**What I think I'm good at**
- I'm creative and can play around with sentences
- I can use strategies to spell unfamiliar words
- I can engage a reader with my stories

**Three things I'd like to improve about my writing**
1 I need to plan my writing more carefully
2 I need to use paragraphs more confidently, especially in non-fiction writing
3 I need to check and edit my writing more thoroughly

**My writing targets**
- To write a paragraph plan for my next major piece of written work in English and to show it to my teacher
- To proofread all of my writing, checking especially for full stops and capital letters

# Myself as a speaker and listener

I don't often put my hand up to answer a question even when I think I know the answer

I get embarrassed when I have to speak in front of the class

I enjoy working in small groups

I'm good at listening to other people's points of view

I enjoy drama activities, especially role play and hot seating. It's as if I can pretend I'm somebody else so I don't feel silly

I usually have quite a definite point of view about things I feel strongly about

I can't always think of something to say

I enjoy listening to stories and have quite a collection of story tapes

Sometimes I mumble and speak too quietly

I recently took part in a class assembly – I was nervous but had spent ages preparing and rehearsing my part. It went quite well

# TASK

Make a mind map for yourself like the one opposite. Then draw out your strengths as a speaker and listener as well as the areas you would like to develop. The following ideas might help you:

**What I think I'm good at**
- I'm good at collaborating in small groups
- I'm confident with drama activities, especially role play
- I can express a point of view strongly

**Three things I'd like to improve about my speaking and listening**
1. I'd like to be more confident when speaking in class
2. I'd like to improve my spoken presentation skills
3. I'd like to be able to develop my answers which tend to be quite short

**My speaking and listening targets**
- To work with a partner to plan and present a short presentation to the class on ways we could improve our school environment
- To answer a question in class at least twice a week for the next two weeks

# SMART targets

## Specific

A vague target such as 'I want to be a better reader' will not help you. Make your targets specific, for example, 'I will spend half an hour reading before I go to bed each evening.'

## Measurable

How will you know whether you have achieved your target? A specific target such as 'I will read a new novel each month' will be easy to measure. Your teacher will also be able to help you.

## Achievable

Make sure that you do not set yourself targets that are beyond your reach at the moment. Take things a step at a time. If you are a Level 4 reader and you want to be Level 6 next month, that is probably a little unrealistic; you will end up feeling demotivated. Set your sights just a little higher than where you are at the moment.

## Relevant

Make sure that the target you set yourself is appropriate for you. Do not aim to read more fiction if it is really non-fiction that you are struggling with.

## Time-bonded

We are all very good at putting things off and there are some jobs that just never seem to get done! Make sure that you set yourself a reasonable time limit, for example, 'By Christmas I will have joined my local library and visited it at least once a fortnight.'

# Remember – be SMART!